ONE FAMILY'S WAR

ONE FAMILY'S WAR

MURIEL GANE PUSHMAN

TEMPUS

I dedicate this book to my dearest children, Margaret, Timothy, Nigel and Ross, who have all given me enormous pleasure.

First published 2006

Tempus Publishing Limited
The Mill, Brimscombe Port,
Stroud, Gloucestershire, GL5 2QG
www.tempus-publishing.com

© Muriel Gane Pushman, 2006

The right of Muriel Gane Pushman to be identified as the Author
of this work has been asserted in accordance with the
Copyrights, Designs and Patents Act 1988.

British Library Cataloguing in Publication Data.
A catalogue record for this book is available from the British Library.

ISBN 0 7524 4006 3

Typesetting and origination by Tempus Publishing Limited
Printed in Great Britain

CONTENTS

ACKNOWLEDGEMENTS

An extra special thank you to my daughter, Margaret, who types my manuscripts so beautifully.

COVER IMAGES

Front cover, above: This picture was taken on Muriel's sister Audrey's wedding day in 1945. Muriel's husband George is on the left; then June Atterbury; Muriel; Christopher Sneath, aged six, and his sister Jane, aged three. The happy couple were Hugh Marcellus Smith Junior and Audrey, just nineteen by two days, and Irving Gane and Ruth Ellis are also in the picture.

Below left: Timothy, Nigel and Margaret Pushman.

Below right: Muriel, with friend Sgt Pat Miller, May 1942.

Back cover, above: Warren Farm House, surrounded by 180 acres of land when Muriel lived there. The upstairs window shown in this photograph was Muriel's bedroom window. The man was Old Thomas, who cut the hay with a scythe.

Below: George and Muriel Pushman leave St Bartholomew's The Great Church in the City of London after their wedding on 14 August 1943. The guard of honour were from RAF Brize Norton. Muriel was a section officer stationed there in the WAAF at that time.

1

A COMFORTABLE LIFE

For a granny to be surrounded by her grandchildren is a gift, by far more precious than gold. So it was for me on a particularly glorious day in June 1989. I had taken my deck chair into a quiet corner of our lovely garden beneath an ancient pear tree, where I could hear their voices and yet was far enough away to close my eyes and pinch forty winks!

The chatter of the young is enchanting, sweetness itself one moment, a raging fury the next, and arguments about whose turn it is to do this and that become a matter of life and death. On these occasions they would rush to my side, whereupon I would listen and then be expected, like Solomon, to pass judgement, whence all would return to sweetness once more. How I loved these rare moments, for I knew only too well that days rush into months and then years, and suddenly these rapturous moments would be but memories.

On this particular day they were engrossed in making a den in the hollow of an old dead oak tree, thus freeing me from my judiciary duties. I therefore permitted myself a little daydreaming, and leaning back I half closed my eyes and gazed up at the blue, blue sky through the tracery of the black twigs of the pear tree, and my memories all came flooding back, as though it had been yesterday.

Yes, I thought, the summer of 1939 had been exactly like this summer, clear blue skies day after day, very, very warm, and yes, even the childish chatter, only then it was the chatter of my little sister Diana, who was five years old and my constant shadow. Yes, that summer was warm and peaceful for the three girls in the Gane family some fifty years ago.

Let me tell you all about my family, during what was to become a momentous and unforgettable time. The fears of war lurking in the minds of our parents never entered our heads, for we were of the generation of children in front of whom things unpleasant, or frightening, were never discussed – least of all the prospect of war.

Our summers were spent, as all our summers had been spent, riding our horses and ponies, entering gymkhanas, swimming and playing tennis. The month of August was set apart for the annual family holiday spent away at the seaside in Suffolk – a positive Peter Pan's Never, Never Land called Thorpeness, where everyone knew everyone else. Here life-long friendships were formed. My husband, years later, described it perfectly as the 'Upper Class Butlins'! What a life you might say – and I'd agree wholeheartedly, it was a wonderful life, but somehow we took it all for granted, for this was the pattern of a typical upper class family of those times, the only difference being the venue of the seaside holiday.

We went by car, packed in like sardines, and I remember my father commenting that if he opened the door not only would a bag of oranges roll out, but the cat would whizz out and end up charging across a ten-acre field into the back of beyond with him (my poor father) in hot pursuit! Indeed I recall one particular journey when the poor cat Tiddles decided in desperation that he needed to relieve himself – and he was wedged on my lap at the time! All the hampers of linen and trunks went ahead by train, it really was so exciting. There were our parents, my widowed grandmother, the family nanny called Flo, her sister Nellie who was our cook and we three girls, plus the family dogs and cat – oh, and the bag of oranges!

My father always took the same house. It was ideal for a family holiday, for apart from us, they always invited a host of friends and my mother always prided herself that she was a cunning match-maker – and she was! I recall several occasions when we girls had to vacate our bedrooms in order to accommodate some unsuspecting bachelor and a free and unattached spinster! My father always drummed it into his daughters that he didn't want them to marry for marrying sake, but he did hold the opinion that a week or month over the age of twenty-five would be pushing our luck and reducing our chances of wedlock considerably. So you can imagine my parents' great joy when they invited our doctor down to Thorpness to meet my father's cousin Mary, who had really been pushing her luck, having reached the grand old age of thirty-four! However, Cupid struck with his arrow, and the knot was tied, and we became bridesmaids at a posh society wedding in London.

To set the scene, let me begin by describing this family – my family: Sir Irving Gane was at that time a solicitor in London, following in the footsteps of his father and grandfather before him. His office, utterly Dickension, was in the Temple in the City of London overlooking the river Thames. Everyone seemed perfectly content to 'know their place', from the chief clerk right down to the office boy, and instead of wall-to-wall carpeting I recall that it was floor to ceiling documents and deeds tied neatly in Barbara Cartland pink solicitors' tape. What has always stayed clearly in my mind is that, despite the pecking order syndrome, my father always treated them with courtesy and great concern for their well-being, and they in turn were totally loyal to him in every respect. Had you passed him in the street in those days his appearance would have given the clue to his occupation, stiffly starched white collar, discreet tie, striped trousers, a black jacket, black homburg or bowler hat, and of course the tightly rolled umbrella! This really was the elite uniform worn by all professionals in the City in those far away days.

His wife, Monty, perhaps did not quite conform to the image one is immediately forming of this man and his family, for she was a Canadian by birth, whose parents had arrived in Canada as teenagers from County Tyrone in Northern Ireland in the last century. She was so delightfully un-English, with a wonderful sense of fun and zany sense of humour. She was petite and very pretty with an eighteen-inch waist of which she was very proud! She had trained as a nurse, and then sailed for England to join the Queen Alexandra's Army Nursing Corps as a theatre sister in 1915. Despite her appearance she was as strong as an ox, fearless and extremely resilient; she was incredibly funny and we loved her for it. However, she ran the family a little on the grounds of a well-run hospital, clinical would best describe it. She adored her children, and when she died my father chose as her epitaph a quotation from *The Economy of Human Life*: 'The care of her family was her whole delight.' She showed tremendous loyalty to my father, but at the same time never feared to debunk him from time to time, thus bringing him down to size whenever she felt he was getting a bit pompous. She always impressed upon us, almost as soon as we could walk, to be sure that we married Canadians, so that we could luxuriate in warm bathrooms and centrally heated houses, for the one thing she never came to terms with was the cold 'English barns' that we happily called houses. Again, this was a typically English approach to those days, stiff upper lips and teeth a-chattering, for one to be healthy meant that the house had to be full of fresh air, and the colder the better, winter and summer alike. If you were cold you just went and put on another woolly, and sat beside a big fire, which invariably meant your front was practically on fire and your back was freezing! I seem to remember that we actually had two radiators in our house, both in the hallways, one upstairs and one down – what luxury! Central heating, my father would say, was for the sissies in our society! I suppose in a way we thought nothing of it, for what you don't know you don't miss.

We certainly had no central heating at boarding school, where sash windows were flung open, as wide as they would go, 365 days of the year. The North Sea was only a stone's throw away, one could almost feel the icy seaspray on our faces in bed at night.

Each morning we had to take a cold bath, which our matron used to run the night before, a masochist if ever there was one, she would stand beside the bath and as one girl would follow another into this icy nightmare she would give us a hefty push to make certain that our shoulders went below the 'plumb line'. After this, shivering with cold and shock, we would dash back to our dormitories and proceed to pile on layer upon layer of clothing, all made of pure wool.

Anyone reading this now would simply find it too incredible to believe, but that is the way things were in the late 1920s. I really find that I can hardly believe it myself, but here goes, from the inside out! Combinations, what on earth were those you may well ask? They were a vest with elbow-length sleeves and pants, all in one, with an opening at the back for obvious reasons, the legs ended just above the knees, with buttons all down the front, quite ghastly, but a veritable green-house! I remember that for parties the sleeves had to be neatly rolled up and then stitched in order that they did not show below the puffed sleeves of our party dresses. There was never any question of leaving the 'combs' off just for a party, heaven forbid we would have to run the risk of catching double pneumonia. On top of the 'combs' we wore a liberty bodice, which really was a sleeveless vest, with buttons on each side for us to hook our suspenders onto, to hold up our thick brown woollen stockings. We wore two pairs of knickers, firstly cotton linings which were topped by thick brown woollen kneelength knickers with a pocket on the leg to pop a hankie into. The viyella blouse and the tie came next, followed by a brown wool gaberdine gym tunic, a v-necked school sweater and last, but not least, our school blazer – how could I ever complain of feeling the cold? I do remember, however, that some girls suffered from terrible chilblains on their fingers and toes, and they used to wear knitted mittens – catching a netball in the wintertime was pure hell for them.

My parents had three daughters. I, Muriel, was their first born, fol-lowed five years later by my sister Audrey, and eight years later Diana joined the family. From the day she arrived she was a firecracker, and I'm certain that she came out of the same mould as my mother, gutsy and quite fearless. The age gaps were unfortunate for it meant that we had very little in common as youngsters. I had ruled the roost for five glorious years, being the apple of my parent's eye, when suddenly a sister arrived, causing me to throw my dog Spot, who was, at the time, my very dearest friend, out of our kitchen window, for which I received a hefty spanking. My jealousy knew no bounds, I was totally mixed up and very miserable, and the insult of all insults was to be sent away to boarding school at the very tender age of six and a half, making me feel more out in the cold than ever.

But fate was kind and I soon settled in, cold baths and all, and I have to admit that I was extremely happy at this little prep school called St Monica's at Kingsdown, near Deal, in Kent. My sisters followed in turn, and that part of our lives was lived very much according to the upper class book!

A great passion in my young life was for my dolls. I had an enormous family of them and lived in a world of dreams. I loved playing hospitals, using my father as the doctor on his return from his office, and I would be allowed to dress up in my mother's wartime nursing sister's uniform, it really was a tremendous treat. In the summertime I would cart my doll family out into our garden to play schools or mothers and fathers. I am always so grateful to have been allowed to remain a child in my imaginative world for as long as I cared to; it is a precious gift, and was for me a wonderfully happy time.

Diana's childhood was far removed from mine, for she was born at a time when the world became topsy turvey, and to survive, she, along with the rest of her generation, had to run before they could walk. Being born in the mid-thirties she became a wartime child at the age of five, deprived of seaside holidays and pretty clothes. Sweets were strictly rationed, she never saw a banana, let alone tasted one and, to crown it all, her father was away from home in the Army and her secure home was suddenly bulging with strangers. All these factors caused her to grow up all too quickly, and consequently she became old beyond her years. By the age of seven she was killing and plucking chickens for our family consumption. She learnt to milk our four cows, Buttercup, Snowdrop, Bluebell and Daisy and even told my mother when they required the services of a bull! In later years she married an Australian from the outback and without doubt her early introduction to life on a farm helped her enormously to adapt to life in the Australian bush.

Our family estate lay nestled between the undulating folds of the Surrey Downs. We had just over 180 acres, with the Pilgrims Way winding its ancient path just behind our fields. It was said that our farmhouse, Warren Farm House, was an inn in Chaucer's time when he wrote The Canterbury Tales, and pilgrims in their hundreds walked from Winchester to Canterbury Cathedral to pay homage at Thomas a Becket's shrine. Whatever it had been in the past really did not matter, for it was to us a very dear house, long and low, with beams to crack your head on, and floors that somehow ran away with you they sloped so. There were nooks and crannies, little attics and a spooky old cellar. Cupboards you could play hide and seek in, and a special little dark cupboard reserved for the cats to have their kittens in as, after all, we did have, at any one time, seventeen cats! This naturally meant that there were always kittens, all shades of the rainbow as you can imagine, and we girls would never allow any to be put to sleep. If homes could not be found for them then, simply, we kept them. King Edward VIII's wife, the infamous Wallis Simpson, was making headline news at the time, which prompted us to name many of our kittens after her, poor things; there were many variations on the theme – Wallis, Wally, Simpson, Simpkins to mention but a few. Their dormitories were out in our barns and stables.

Our dog population was a little smaller, four at the start of the war, increasing to seven, and constantly fluctuating to fourteen whenever puppies were around. They were all tremendous characters, for we never owned a pedigree. We usually acquired them when having a quick walk around the Guildford cattle market. We would make a beeline for the dog pens to see what was on offer, when suddenly we would espy a pen of unhappy looking little pups, and that was it! 3s 6d was all that was required to purchase one of these forlorn little creatures. As our pocket money was only 1s 3d per week, we had to manage a fair amount of juggling to go shares, so that the deal could be cinched – what joy as we arrived home with a fat little bundle of charm in our arms. My mother nearly had fifty fits, but secretly, I think she loved them as much as we did. The trouble was that precious little thought was ever given into wondering what they might grow up to look like. Pluto was a mixture of spaniel and golden retriever, and a gentleman in anyone's language. Towser, who was one part Jack Russel and fifty-six parts anyone's guess, always kept one leg off the ground – why we never knew, but he still managed to run like the wind ahead of the other three. One-eyed Nick had obviously been kicked as a puppy, and had a rather unpleasant bulging blind eye, but was an absolute darling without a nasty thought in his head, despite man's brutality towards him. We had a beagle called Puppet, and Pete, a small cairn, and Robbie, who was a black cocker spaniel – the list goes on and on.

The main purpose of having our land was to graze our horses, which were kept purely for the family's pleasure and what a pleasure this turned out to be. My father's first purchase was an Icelandic pony called Stjarni, which is Icelandic for 'Star'. He happened to mention to a friend in the City that he planned to find a quiet pony for his daughters. His friend assured him that an Icelandic pony was just the thing, safe, steady, and utterly reliable. The excitement in our family was tremendous, when we were told that we were to have a pony of our very own. On the day that he was due we all went down to Guildford station to await his arrival. He had cost the vast sum of £6 and his journey from Iceland to Leith in Scotland, followed by the long train journey to Guildford, must have been quite an ordeal for him. As we waited excitedly on the platform we fully expected him to be led out of a cattle wagon, but nothing doing, for some unknown reason he was led out of the first class baggage compartment walking like a king! My father said that this last part of the journey had cost twice as much as the pony himself!

He was quite adorable and looked just like a woolly bear, his coat was incredibly thick and a lovely shade of conker brown. His mane was thick too, very shaggy coarse hair completely covering his large brown eyes. Oh, how we loved him on sight. We realised that he was unable to understand one single word we were saying, and we certainly had no knowledge of the Icelandic language, but we gave him enough hugs, pats and kisses to make up for any loss of conversation.

In the early days he proved to be the very devil to catch. Every time we approached him he would craftily turn his hind quarters towards us, one foot would be nonchalantly poised, part hoof off the ground and although he never kicked, we always had the feeling that he just might! So it took a lot of time, patience and gentle persuasion to sort him out.

Soon after his arrival we planned to enter him in our very first gymkhana, and because of his tremendously thick coat my father decided to clip him. He fixed up the electric clippers and set to work. After a few minutes Stjarni began kicking out furiously and seemed to be most unhappy. My father and Dick, the young groom we employed, couldn't understand what could be causing Stjarni to act in such a peculiar manner, so my father said to Dick, 'Put your fingers on these clippers.' Dick did, and nearly shot out of the stables, for it appeared that the clippers were live. By this time Stjarni was looking a complete mess, for my father was just running the clippers over him in a willy-nilly fashion, and somehow or other the job had to be completed – but how? My father had a brilliant idea, 'Muriel darling, go in to mummy and get her to come out with four large Wellington boots.' Whatever does he want those for, I wondered, but was soon to find out. He shoved Stjarni's four legs down into the boots, and Bob's your uncle, Stjarni was insulated! You have never seen such an amusing sight, but the job was successfully completed, with no further shocks, and our pony looked resplendent, and walked away from the show with his first of many red rosettes.

In order that we could go for family rides, Lorna, a chestnut mare, was purchased for my father to ride, and I couldn't believe my good fortune when Sally, a part Arab mare was given to me on my birthday. She was a beauty and knew it! I was of an age when girls, if they ride and have ponies of their own, tend to make this hobby their main interest. This certainly was the case with me, for Sally and I became inseparable for many years. We rode as a family every morning before breakfast, and at weekends we would take long rides, sometimes lasting the better part of the day, taking with us a packed lunch. Our dogs would come with us as a matter of course and they could be seen in a single file snaking behind us, always with dear old three-legged dot and fetch it Towser bringing up the rear. However, after a couple of miles he would pack it in and slink off home to the blissful warmth of his basket in front of the kitchen fire.

As children we accepted this routine as normal and never considered querying it. It was, I suppose, a way of life and we were just content to go along with it, we were after all divinely happy.

Our school holidays were fully occupied on the farm preparing our ponies for horse shows. We had to map out and plan our routes to get to these shows, for we were certainly never transported there in a horse box. We rode with our friends across the Surrey Downs, meandering through primrose and bluebell woods, never really having to cross a main road for mile upon mile. Our daily chores were to muck out the stables and the never ending cleaning of our tack. Our friends shared our interests – my special friend, who lived next door, was Joan Grant. This meant that life in our mid-teens was very, very happy, and occupied to the full.

Being a family of girls meant that boys did not really register in those early days, in fact we only met them on the rarest of occasions. I recall the Easter holidays in 1938, I was to have extra coaching for the forthcoming School Certificate examinations. My father sent me to a cramming school run by a retired Army colonel at his home in Guildford. His manner was somewhat brusque and indeed a little frightening, I thought as he showed me into the workroom. Upon entering I nearly had fifty fits, for apart from one empty chair, to become mine, the room was a sea of male faces, all grinning and smiling with the odd wink thrown in for good measure. Being female I soon recovered and realised that the next two weeks were going to be fun, if nothing else. This was the turning point in my life and a time when my beloved horse Sally started to have to take the slightest of back seats, with her tack only getting a quick spit and polish instead of hours of tender loving care.

There were fifteen young men staying with the colonel. Most came from Europe, they were older than I and had come to learn English. It was well-nigh impossible to reserve my love for just one of them. One was utterly spoilt for choice, my emotions were in a constant whirl. Looking back, they were such innocent emotions, there was no bed hopping – that just never came into things, boys then had been brought up to behave like gentlemen. Of course there was the inevitable cad, and the over-hormoned maiden, but by and large we just had love affairs that were fun.

I had never met a foreign boy before, so what with their broken English, coupled with their impeccable manners, they were so enchanting. Chocolates for me when taken out, and a king-sized gold wicker basket with an enormous handle, topped by a frothy pink ribbon which overflowed into a positive rainbow of flowers for my mother, no doubt to soften her up to allow me to go out with them! How could she refuse, she was as captivated as I was! Not so my father; his Victorian ways, high moral code of behaviour and his strong in-built suspicion of foreigners (especially those wanting to take out his daughter) made him all the more determined to keep a watchful eye on these boys at the colonel's house!

He insisted upon accompanying us to dances, and would while away the evening reading in the library until it was time for the festivities to draw to a close. Years later he said that he could never be certain that the Spaniard didn't keep a dagger down his sock. How that Spaniard would have laughed had he known my father's thoughts – for he was a young Spanish count, with a glorious name, Count Alberto Dibos de Menchaca, devastatingly handsome. Come to think of it, he may well have kept a dagger down his sock, for he kept telling me, with black eyes flashing, that he would kill the gentle French boy, Guy, if I continued swimming with him!

There were a few English boys on the course, one of whom I shall never forget. He was knee-high to a grasshopper and he would keep following me around like a puppy dog. I couldn't be doing with it, mainly I think because he was such a shorty and I happened to be so tall and willowy – the 'Mutt and Jeff' cartoons seemed to loom constantly in my mind. How strange the priorities of youth.

Little had I realised in those happy carefree Easter holidays that the threat of a war was so close and that these boys, like all of our own British boys, would be fighting for their very existence. Or that I would be plucked from the security of my serene and sheltered home to become one of the thousands of girls in uniform.

2

DISTANT THUNDER

It was obvious that war was imminent, one could tell by the wireless and newspapers and simply by listening to the grown-ups' conversations but still I really couldn't grasp what it was going to involve. A friend telephoned me to ask if I would go and help at the Town Hall taking details from people who came in their hundreds to offer their services in one way or another, or to offer accommodation and homes for evacuee children should the grim necessity ever arise. It was only a small voluntary job, but it made me feel part of a very big task force in the making.

In the evenings, I, along with many other teenagers, would go to the local factory to help in the assembling of gas masks. We were all given set pieces to join together, just like a wooden jigsaw puzzle. Someone would brew tea, and the atmosphere was happy and carefree, despite the grim and fearsome undertones. I never stopped to think of the horror of a gas attack, or the fact that one of these gas masks in the making would have to go everywhere with me for the next six years.

Coming into our house after an exhilarating ride and feeling ravenous for Nellie's super Sunday breakfast of sizzling homebred pork bacon just oozing with fat, with a brace of fresh farm eggs, field mushrooms and fried bread – a breakfast fit for a king – I found my parents huddled around the wireless frantically trying to tune it in, so as to not miss a single word. What can be wrong, I thought, everyone seems to look so serious. Within seconds I was to learn the reason why. It was that fateful Sunday of 3 September 1939, and the time was 11 a.m. precisely. Our Prime Minister, Mr Neville Chamberlain, announced the news that war against Germany had been declared. So this was it, what we had all feared for so long.

When he had finished speaking to the nation, I was left with an eerie hollow in my stomach and for the first time a feeling of panic began to creep from my toes to the top of my head. As I looked around the room our beloved father was already making plans to return to the Army. What would happen to my mother, I wondered – if she goes back to nursing who's going to look after us, the house and the estate? Oh, what a wretched mess – our whole life is being turned upside down.

At that time my sister Audrey was far from well with a form of ulcerative colitis, and Diana was only five years old. Our nanny, Flo, was the mainstay of the family, along with her sister Nellie, our cook, they were woven into our life's tapestry, we loved and needed them dearly. The animals, gosh, how we loved them too, would there be sufficient food to feed them? I was near to tears as suddenly a new horror struck me, what if the Germans should be dropped by para-chutes this very day, on the sacred land of Warren Farm House. I was only too aware of the brutality they handed out to the Jews in Germany, it had been all too plain to see on newsreels at the cinema, where once again I had cocooned myself in cotton wool and smugly thought that it could never happen on British soil.

I even detected fear in the eyes of my parents, they were talk-ing quietly together, and I wished that I could hear fully what they were saying – what was that? Getting rid of our cars, including our magnificent week-old Super Humber Snipe, this, my father said, he would offer to the Army for Staff Officers' usage. He was talking like a machine gun – increase the number of cows, pigs, chickens – possibly have to consider selling our horses and ponies – plan for the pos-sibility of food shortages – they just seemed to go on and on, totally unaware that the eldest of their daughters was trying to catch every word, words which were frightening her to death. Things certainly were changing, and changing fast – what would tomorrow bring?

As usual, I drove my father down to the railway station in Guildford the next morning in his beloved old 'Puffing Billy'. Now Puffing Billy was a vintage Austin 10, 1927. I could write a separate story about him alone and all his adventures. En route my father tried to put my mind at rest and as an afterthought as he got out of the car, told me what I should do if the air-raid warning siren were to go off whilst I was driving the car. With that we kissed goodbye and away he went.

I had no sooner driven out of the station forecourt, when off went the air-raid siren, the very first so far as Guildford was concerned, and only 8 a.m. in the morning. I tried not to panic, but I was terribly afraid, everyone was running helter skelter, air-raid wardens and policemen just seemed to pop up out of the ground, frantically waving at everyone to take shelter. I was two miles away from my home and began driving like a lunatic. I had not been driving all that long and in my fright I was crashing the gears. At last a policeman stepped out into the road, he and I seemed to be the only people left in the world. He stopped me, no doubt just as frightened as I was, telling me to get out immediately and dash into the nearest house. I don't recall turning my engine off such was my panic.

The area was a very rundown part of Guildford, mean little shops and Victorian terraced villas with the gasworks situated bang opposite and station yards all around. I was virtually pushed in through the door to find I was crammed into a tiny room just bulging with people standing around, bewildered, frightened, but as always on these occasions, silent. A dear frail old soul, obviously the tenant, was making a pot of tea, which she passed around. I shall never forget the taste of that tea, for from then on a crisis without the tea being brewed up and passed around was unheard of.

The minutes ticked away and I, no doubt along with everyone else in that little room, wondered what was about to happen to us all. My thoughts darted crazily from one subject to another – my father on his train for London, I imagined that they would be sure to bomb trains. Then, my mother, in charge of her family at the farm. My sisters, would they be frightened too, I wondered? Poor Nellie was as deaf as a post, and would want a running commentary just so she could be kept in the picture. Flo was a tower of strength, but then, what about my elderly grandmother? My Aunt Lilah, and then the thought struck me – would they be worrying about me and my whereabouts? Oh no, I suddenly realised we were in a house opposite the gas holders, and they would surely have a go at bombing those, all three of them, in which case everyone in this stark little room would be blown to smithereens. Please, dear Lord, I prayed earnestly, don't let this happen today, by tomorrow, I kept telling myself over and over again, I shall be under control, and won't allow myself to give way to my fear. I then looked around the room and saw that the silence that had come over everyone meant that they too were probably every bit as frightened as I. In a strange way it was comforting, and compassion grew out of fear of the unknown that very first day of the war.

Suddenly, the shrill clear sound of the 'All Clear' filled the air and in an instant everybody relaxed and broad smiles spread across their faces – mine too. We thanked the dear old lady who had given us shelter and were then allowed to leave. Yes, I had left the engine running, but who cared? I was alive, so now for home – top speed. In thirty minutes I, Muriel Gane, grew up.

My father joined the Army and MI5 within the week. My mother was to have the biggest task of all – to keep the home fires burning, along with thousands of other women, some of whom were to manage better than others. My mother, who had the strength of an ox, the determination of Sir Winston Churchill and the courage of Nelson, would not only keep the home fires burning, but would run the farm, collect the pigswill from peoples' houses like a dustman, have a house bulging with evacuees and keep open house for over 1,000 Canadian servicemen who were 3,000 miles away from their homes. She nursed my sick sister Audrey, cared for my grandmother and ancient Aunt Lilah – coped with two floods and six bombs – just for starters. She was to keep morale high when others were pessimistic, and I am sure that the tremendous stresses suffered, but never shown, were responsible for her premature death in 1951 aged fifty-nine years. If anyone deserved a medal, she did.

3

WAR

We had now accepted the fact that we were all at war. The mood of the nation had changed completely within the first three weeks. Everyone wanted to become involved in one way or another. We saw our neighbours rushing to enlist in the Armed Services or, if they were unfit or too old for the services then there was an enormous range of options; the Home Guard or 'Dad's Army', the Fire Service, Observer Corps and Air-Raid Wardens to name but a few – all equally vital and desperate for volunteers.

It was strange to see people that we had known all our lives suddenly looking quite different and a little self conscious in their new uniforms, and whether it was the war or the uniform or perhaps a little bit of both, it put pep into their step. Why, I clearly remember an elderly neighbour who had suffered for years with arthritis suddenly becoming upright and striding out with a purpose, his stick was nowhere to be seen, and with his cap tilted at a saucy angle he was ready to tackle anything!

My friends' mothers all joined the Red Cross, St John's Ambulance Brigade or the WVS and they too found a new lease of life, with new-found freedom away from the confines of their homes. I've a sneaking feeling that it tickled their egos no end to be chatted up by soldiers in canteens, who more often than not were just plain home-sick and missing their own families.

We had endless visits from officials, all anxious for details on how many people were living in the house, could we possibly take more? Perhaps nurses from the local hospital, the Army, or even evacuee children? Had we a suitable place in the house to turn into an air-raid shelter in case of air raids? Advice was offered on how to go about re-enforcing with sandbags. The seriousness of the situation was being brought home to us in no uncertain terms.

We had visits from the War Agricultural Committee with detailed plans for my father to put his small estate onto a wartime footing. Fields to be ploughed up and turned over to corn production, potatoes and the rearing of bullocks for starters. My father, so anxious to comply, agreed willingly with all their schemes and then promptly went off to work for MI5, leaving my dear mother to produce the goods, despite the fact that she didn't know one end of a bullock from another!

My older friends were joining the Women's Services and I desperately wanted to join up too, but had to wait until I had left college. I always remember with envy my friend's sister, Betty, joining the WAAF. All she was given in those early days in the form of uniform was an airforce blue raincoat, a beret and grey stockings and was told to report to West Drayton for training.

My father was in MI5 and working at the War Office, however his office was in the strangest and most secure of places – being a cell inside Wormwood Scrubs Prison! We only saw him occasionally, as he found it impracticable to commute on a daily basis.

Audrey had by this time become seriously ill and had to be admitted to St Thomas's Hospital in London, where she remained for several weeks in the children's ward, this alone was a great worry to my parents. Guildford was beginning to liven up considerably. St Thomas's Hospital transferred the main part of their medical school to the two hospitals in Guildford, so despite the fact that our local friends were leaving to join the services, a new force of chaps was arriving.

I still had one constant thought on my mind, to join up, but I knew deep down that my parents would never hear of it; somehow it fell into the same category as wanting to become a dancer on the stage, which, when I suggested that, caused my father to turn a sickly shade of green. He genuinely thought he had come up with a good compromise when he sent me off to a physical training college.

The billeting officer sent along a young medical student in need of somewhere to live, he was not only charming, but handsome in a British sort of way, his name was Tony Howarth and he came from Sussex. He asked my mother if she minded if he brought his horse to live alongside our horses at the farm. She was always a soft touch, and so Silver came to swell our already large menagerie. There seemed to be an endless stream of students in the house visiting Tony, and they always seemed to be hungry, thank goodness we had bacon, eggs and milk in plenty in those early months to fill their appetites. It was indeed a happy winter and the horror of things to come did not really hit the young ones at Warren Farm House.

Following our medical student, an Army colonel and his wife were billeted on us, two nurses who worked on different shifts and twin evacuees from the East End of London, the dockland area. They were the children of a docker, and a right pair of cheeky ones they turned out to be. Helen and John, aged seven, were just oozing with cockney wit and our nanny Flo was far from being best pleased to begin with. However, within the first month they had won her over and she became as pliable as a piece of putty in their hands.

Try to picture my mother and Nellie organising the food to sustain this expanding tribe. The house just bulged at the seams – beds had been found amidst cobwebs and inches of dust at the back of the attic and bedding had been supplied by the WVS. We girls had to double up; I now shared my room with Diana, not a rip roaring success, because she insisted on having her pet mouse Brownie in the bedroom. I am simply not a lover of these furry creatures, especially not when it escaped from its cage and found its way into my lingerie drawer – ugh!

Nellie was a saint, she never got into a flap and managed, rather like Jesus Christ, to stretch the food designed to feed five to accommodate 5,000. Food in those far away days was far more simple and probably more wholesome than it is today. On average a main course was served, followed by, as my father would refer to them, 'One of Nellie's workhouse puddings'! A good corner filler, like a steamed or boiled treacle roly-poly pudding, spotted dick, or rice pudding – we enjoyed them and always cleared our plates to the last crumb.

Great excitement came one summer's night, all was silence, we had gone to bed when we were suddenly rudely awakened by loud banging on the front door. What on earth was wrong I wondered, was the enemy at the door? We all came sleepy-eyed out of our bedrooms like the little wooden figures in a weather house. As always, it was my mother who was first down the stairs, pulling her dressing gown on as she rushed in the direction of the banging. Upon opening the door she was confronted by a motley bunch of the Home Guard. If you have ever watched *Dad's Army* on the television then you can picture the scene on our doorstep. 'What on earth is wrong?' asked my mother. All in a chorus they told her excitedly that they suspected German parachutists had landed in one of our fields at the back of our vegetable garden. They told her that they had been sent to investigate a series of blue flashing lights – possibly some form of communication between the parachutists – and it was definitely coming from our field. 'Now madam, we want you to take your family upstairs, locking all the doors as you go, and bedroom doors if possible, we are off to investigate, so don't open the door to anyone until we come back' and with that they shuffled off into the night. The suggestion that we should lock all our doors was unknown to us, for in those far away days one seldom even locked the front door – perhaps only when we went on our annual holiday.

To say that we were scared out of our wits would have been the understatement of the century, we were terrified. Flo was flapping around like a demented hen rounding up her charges. Nellie hadn't heard a word and pleaded with all or anyone to tell her what on earth had happened. Granny had come from her end of our house with Aunt Lilah, who had the misfortune to look like an old Red Indian Squaw – she wore her white hair parted in the centre with a couple of pigtails hanging on either side of her face. She had very bushy black eyebrows, a moustache and she wore a permanent scowl – to finish the picture she wrapped around herself an Indian rug! Granny on the other hand was my best friend, she was tall, elegant and intelligent, and so young at heart, everyone loved her. But how could we not be frightened? We went upstairs, but no one felt like locking themselves away behind their bedroom doors, so we just pathetically hovered around waiting to see what would develop, with the comforting knowledge that the Home Guard were mounting guard around the property. In a way, deep down it was exciting, for the war had actually arrived on our very own doorstep.

Imagine our relief when the familiar banging on the front door was heard. This time we all rushed downstairs to find a sheepish and extremely apologetic bunch of old boys telling us of the night's drama. The electrical equipment they had been sent to find never materialised, for it transpired that as they were crawling up the field on their bellies they had not noticed a thin wire stretching across the field, one of them had touched it with his backside, nearly catapulting him up to the stars. It was all we could do to keep our faces straight, for we knew what was coming, they were a dear old bunch of gentlemen, after all intent only on doing their duty, and on this particular night it was to protect us. What they had touched was our electric fence which we used to keep our cows from straying!

It was a few days before Christmas, when the preparations were in full swing, that we read in the newspapers of the arrival of the first contingent of the Canadian Forces. My mother had already mentioned that she would like nothing better than for the farmhouse to become 'Open House' to Canadian boys far from home, but I don't think she had anticipated that they would be taking her up on her offer so soon.

On Christmas Eve there was a loud knock at the front door, it was a wild and windy night I well remember, and standing on the doorstep were two very tall and extremely dashing young soldiers. My heart missed a beat, well maybe even two beats when they said 'Hi, you must be Muriel, it's your cousins Jack and Clarence Hallet from Canada.' To be perfectly honest, I had never realised that I had two cousins anywhere, let alone in Canada. My excitement was tremendous, how super to suddenly have two cousins, and just for them to arrive at Christmas time was wonderful. They were both in The Royal Canadian Mounted Police, known and loved by all of us as 'The Mounties'. What, I ask you, could be more romantic for a girl who had always lived in a world of dreams?

This put us all in high spirits, and the festivities continued for several days. It was a full house, for my mother had already arranged to accept six officers to join us on Christmas Day. Luckily we had a large antique dining room table that just seemed to expand in a never-ending fashion. This was our first wartime Christmas, these were our first wartime guests – unknown a year ago yet now very much an integral part of our family. We were so lucky to have this transatlantic influence in our home, for Canadians really love to go to town over Christmas – every little detail is given top priority, from decorating the tree to gift wrapping presents – yes, we were indeed very lucky.

Our turkey was 'home grown'; I tried not to think about it, for our farm animals had always become our friends. The York ham had once been Harold Trotter – I have a strong feeling that one day I shall end up becoming a vegetarian! The table was a picture, formally laid with sparkling antique glasses, crisp white linen napkins, and red and gold table decorations and crackers. It was a particular joy for us all to watch the faces of the little evacuee children, with their never-ending prattle and shining eyes as round as gobstoppers.

Nellie came into her element on Christmas Day, she would be given a glass of port and to see her one would think she had consumed the entire bottle! All inhibitions were cast to the four winds, she would sing, she would hiccough, she would giggle and her *piéce de résistance* was to partake in the party games, her favourite being fishing for a sixpence. What's so odd about that you may ask? Well, a large zinc wash tub with a handle at each end was suspended between two kitchen chairs, this was done by passing a broom handle through the tub handles and then gently positioning this makeshift 'boat' between the two chairs so that it could swing freely. The idea was to gingerly climb into the tub, one leg either side of the broom handle whilst perching one's behind on the very thin and uncomfortable broom stick, this was not an easy task, as the slightest movement sent the entire tub rocking and rolling! A sixpence was then positioned on the floor a small distance away, and with a bendy cane one had to try and stretch very gently to coax the sixpence near enough to the tub to be able to bend over and pick it up. Obviously as soon as one leant off centre the entire tub did a summersault and the participant was thrown out in an undignified heap on the carpet!

Nellie's great act was to hang on for as long as possible and then, with her knickers (always new for this occasion) on show, usually kneelength and bright pink, she would be catapulted out of the tub to resounding cheers and clapping. From that moment onwards there would be no further sign of her, she would retire to her bed to sleep it off. But her contribution was to cook the most fantastic dinner with all the frills before taking her glass of port.

The war seemed a very long way away as we danced to the topical records, some of them such silly songs, but so catchy – *Run, Rabbit, Run* was Diana's favourite, *We're hanging out the washing on the Siegfried Line*, *I like a nice cup of tea in the morning* and *Kiss me goodnight Sergeant Major* – they are now all tucked away safely in my memory box to cherish always. In those days it seems we had a tune for all occasions and I suppose we girls went a little weak at the knees over all the lovely sentimental songs – we were able to associate one of these with a particular memory, for they were all lovely melodies to dance cheek to cheek with our man of the moment. I know I certainly had mine, ones like *Room 504*, *Two sleepy people*, *I'm in the mood for love* and the unforgettable *We'll meet again*, made so poignant by Vera Lynn.

This Christmas saw the beginning of my mother's 'Open House to Canadians' and the word soon spread that there was a lovely old farmhouse tucked away in the folds of the Surrey Downs, where a Canadian lady had opened her doors for all to enter. She was in her element, fussing around them, making sure there were warm log fires for the boys to sit around whilst writing their letters home, and to generally be able to relax. They could always be sure of having ham and eggs, succulent roast chicken, milk from our cows and beer from a large barrel, always on tap!

They showed their appreciation by repairing odd items for her. I recall being 'chatted up' by two officers on a train journey to London, the fare in those days was 6s 8d return, and I happened to mention that our pet turkey Blondie (she was called this as she was pure white, which was unusual because all the other turkeys were a greyish black mixture) had broken her leg. They volunteered with alacrity to come and make a splint for her leg. They were, they said, Canadian doctors in the RCAMC so, much to my mother's amazement down the drive they came in a military jeep, complete with the tools of their trade. They gave dear Blondie a whiff of anaesthetic, the bone was set and splinted, and Blondie flourished to become the pride and joy of my mother's flock. She ended up doing her bit for the war effort, for she was raffled shortly before Christmas at a 'Wings for Victory' coffee morning, and the money she raised must have gone a long way towards buying a propeller for a Spitfire!

These boys showed their appreciation to my mother in so many different ways; they gave her their clothing coupons, and brought delicious goodies sent in their food parcels from Canada. Instead of our house becoming lonely and cheerless as so many houses had become, it became alive and a wonderful place to be, like a very 'exclusive club'!

My teenage love was a boy called Donald. He lived with his parents in a lovely house just further up the hill. He was the youngest in his family and was training to be a solicitor. Our friendship began when we caught the same bus home from school every evening. The shy glances that we exchanged were rarely followed up with conversation – but for some time I loved him dearly from afar! However, once the ice had been broken we became close friends, and he was very much an important part of my life. We played tennis together, danced and picnicked together and spoke for hours at a time on the telephone, much to the annoyance of our parents, who thought it was a wasteful extravagance! But we cared not.

Donald had by now joined the Fleet Air Arm as an Able Seaman, becoming an officer after a few months. He looked so super in his uniform, I melted at the sight of him. He gave me his ABs bell-bottomed trousers when he was commissioned, and with one pair my grandmother managed to make me a pretty nifty skirt out of the wide sections of the trouser legs, and the second pair I wore like a sailor. I felt that I cut a pretty snazzy dash in them – they certainly attracted a lot of attention and wolf whistles, and, truthfully speaking, most of us find that good for our egos! They had, however, one huge problem, the material was coarse and hairy, and one felt the urge to have a good old scratch, but to no avail. This was rectified by adding a silk lining to the skirt, made from an old parachute, which my grandmother dyed with Stephensons blue ink to match the colour of the skirt. It was amazing what one could do if one had to.

Donald was later awarded the DSC and wrote an excellent book entitled *Avenger from the Sky*.

4

A DIFFERENT WORLD

Although life continued, the speed at which we lived it had changed dramatically. It was as though we had all stepped onto a vast treadmill that whirled continuously round and round, never slowing down to allow us to step off, to regain our breath and equilibrium or charge up our batteries – even for a precious few hours before heading off on it again.

The summer days were glorious and nature was living out her set pattern as she has done since time began. The swallows were here and the nightingales were singing their magic notes from our trees at Warren Farm House, luckier than their cousins in Berkeley Square. Yet if one cast one's eye up towards blue skies without a puff of cloud, one could see ballet performed by two silver birds – with exquisite grace, but with murder in their eyes. Twirling and whirling, a ballet with a tragic ending for someone was destined to lose their battle for life – an honour for any son of the mother country, we had been brought up to believe.

The evacuation of Dunkirk was taking place, and I was asked to go down to Guildford railway station to help the WVS give out tea and sandwiches to these poor defeated soldiers as they came through on the troop trains from the sea ports. I shall always remember them, their unshaven faces lined with exhaustion, they were partly clothed and so utterly tired and dejected, but they were so very grateful for a hot cup of tea, the chance to talk, and maybe even grab a quick kiss from a young girl. It seemed so little to offer for the 'all' that they had given. The Guards Regiment for example, although routed and dishevelled, had still managed, with their supreme discipline, to have tidied themselves to the best of their ability and their guns were cleaned and polished. One could only admire their pride which out-shone their defeat.

There were several of us who used to visit the French wounded in hospital in Guildford for they were lonely and needed companion-ship. The fact that our French was of '*la plume de ma tante*' standard really didn't matter. They enjoyed our visits, and many friendships were struck up at the same time. Many had suffered severe burns when their ships had been bombed and sunk, and they had been forced to jump into the sea. The Germans had set fire to the oil floating on the water, the survivors becoming human torches.

My thoughts would often return to my grandmother – we were all young, our lives lay stretched out before us and despite moments of fear and sheer panic, we were after all making history for better or for worse. At times I would dash past my grandmother's windows to see her sitting there all alone, silently gazing up at the carnage taking place in the clear blue summer skies above. I wondered what her thoughts were, for only twenty-two years back in history, her only son had served in the horrendous trench warfare of the First World War, the war they said that was to end all wars. I loved her dearly, so would run upstairs to join her at the window, and so distract her thoughts.

Such was life that summer of 1940, the relentless pattern never changed day in and day out and the numbers killed rose daily. Where was it all going to end? We were now hearing that some of our neighbours' sons were being either killed or taken prisoner. This really brought it home, but still that relentless wheel turned and trag-edy was accepted with astonishing bravery and a watery smile. There was little else one could do.

An act of God can strike at anytime, peacetime and wartime alike, and He certainly dealt us a cruel and unexpected blow the following spring, the effects of which could not have been more catastrophic.

We had had a week of heavy snowfalls making the farm a winter wonderland, and quite exquisitely beautiful. In those far away days before central heating, Jack Frost used to go to work on the glass window panes with his ice paint brush, and his paintings were pictures of fairyland magic – giant forests and hidden dells, frozen lakes and snow capped mountains. I would sit with Diana at the bedroom window and spin her tales of fairy magic, which, I have to admit, I enjoyed as much as she did. We would watch the sun slowly melting the magic away, and I would continue the story another day.

However, after a week of this enchantment there was a sudden thaw. The frozen ground could not cope with all the water, so it gathered from the hillsides along the valley and down it rushed at an ever increasing speed. Our old house straddled the valley and to our horror and disbelief we saw a huge tidal wave roaring down our garden flattening a twelve-foot privet hedge in its wake, as it ruthlessly rushed towards the back of our house. It was too late to take any action, all we could do was to close our eyes and wait for the consequences. The crashing noise was thunderous and our windows and doors shattered like matchsticks as it forced its way in on one side of the house, channelling its way into every nook and cranny, then out and away on its reckless course at the other side, ruthlessly taking with it all the contents of our cupboards. Saucepans, shoes and the dogs, who had been quietly sleeping, now found themselves sailing away in their baskets with expressions of sheer panic on their faces. The apples stored in the cellar were popping up through a smashed floorboard in a crazy fashion, almost as though they were being juggled by an invisible man at a circus. The antique oak blocks of the kitchen floor became loose, and floated out like little boats on the ocean.

By this time we had grabbed whatever we could find to hang onto for grim death, for we were now knee deep in muddy water and very frightened. All was now silent except the quiet gurgle, glug, glug of the subsiding water. We were speechless, and indeed timid in the eyes of God, for surely this violent deed was an act of God, and no human being could combat such an act.

After an hour or so the water had receded, leaving in its wake a thick slimy layer of sludgy mud. Our lovely home was a total wreck and all that one felt like doing was to sit down for a good cry. This was not to be, for my mother had already begun organising the relief campaign. With sleeves rolled up, and still in our soggy clothes, she issued the commands like a general. 'Muriel and Nellie, I want you to go and find the dogs and bring them home, remember to find their baskets and, oh, take a basket with you to collect up the saucepans, floor blocks and anything else you can carry. Later we will search everywhere, make piles and bring them home, we'll harness up Stjarni in the trap, and when you pass the stables have a look at Teena and her puppies to see if they are all right.' What a sad sight we found in the stables, all the pups had been drowned and their mother was demented trying to gather them up. I thought war was cruel, but so was nature on that particular day.

All our goods and chattels had ended up in an old dried up pond, now swollen to bursting point with water way down the valley. The trail of devastation stretched like an angry swathe from our house to this pond, and even our normally burnished saucepans looked pathetically scruffy lying in a bed of mud. The dogs were relieved and thrilled to see us after their ordeal and despite the mud we all hugged one another at being together once more.

By the time we returned home my mother, Flo and the cowman's wife, endearingly known as 'Mrs Bill', had hosed down the entire ground floor, but still there was this soggy, sludgy mud everywhere. We had many Persian rugs and in the task of pulling them outside the house I could imagine what it was like pulling the stones to build Stonehenge – they surely weighed a ton. The piano appeared to be a total wreck, with muddy water belching out of all its nooks and crannies. The sofas and chairs looked damaged beyond repair – what a mess.

We slowly tackled one job after another under my mother's guidance. The bookcase holding the *Encyclopedia Britannica* was jammed solid with mud, the books had swelled, making it impossible to pull them out and with all the will in the world, they were stuck fast. We desperately needed some men with their natural brute force as we simply had not got the strength required to lift and to carry. 'If only father was at home' I said. 'Well he's not' snapped my mother, 'so stop wishing. Let's have a cup of tea, and then we can begin again.' It must have been at least midnight before we all crawled into bed and the cot did not need rocking that night!

Luckily for us the Surrey Downs are chalk, so the water quickly soaked away and, with all the doors and windows left wide open, the house soon began to dry out. The weather at least was kind. The irony was that the house had just recently been painted and re-wall-papered before the outbreak of war, and now, to look at it was quite ghastly, with a muddy tide line about three feet up the walls. It was out of the question to have it redecorated, but I went out and bought some poster paints and did a mural in the dining room. The scene that I painted was of mountains with forests, and, heaven knows why, stampeding elephants! My sister Audrey was to return from hospital to spend nearly two years in bed, in this room, and I always hoped that it would amuse her. Because of her illness when she did come home she had to have her bedroom downstairs, so that we could move her as quickly as possible into our air-raid shelter at the far end of the house. The rest of the house had to remain undecorated until the end of the war, but this was really of little consequence, for the atmosphere was wholeheartedly happy and welcoming, with everyone always 'homing in' on our farm kitchen which was always glowing with warmth.

There was the old farm range in the corner, with a gathering of cats contentedly snoozing or licking their whiskers, intermingled with dogs lazily sprawled out, giving the odd twitch, and dreaming no doubt of rabbits. Nellie's budgies and canaries would be singing their equivalent of 'Madame Butterfly' which necessitated throwing a blanket over the top of their cages to shut them up, thus preserving our sanity.

The windows had to be totally blackened out at night throughout the land, to avoid detection by the enemy. Here we were fortunate at the farm, for being a very old house, wooden shutters had been fixed to the inside of all these windows centuries ago. This did not only do the trick of blacking out, but they also helped to keep out the cold. As a double safeguard we then pulled special heavy cotton blackout curtains, before finally pulling our own normal curtains.

There was an antique pine kitchen table and chairs, old and worn by years of usage thus giving a dull shine to the wood. There was an old horsehair one-ended sofa, more often than not covered with white dog hairs from our old friend Towser, who would craftily nip up there for forty winks when nobody was in the kitchen. The ceiling was beamed and not designed for the tall amongst us. One of the cupboards there, as I mentioned earlier, had become a permanent crèche for kittens.

Out of sight, around the corner, the two-ring gas stove was constantly on the go, cooking up the pigswill and chicken scraps in two huge galvanized pails. Hopefully the smell was more appealing to the farmyard animals than we human beings, for it most certainly could never be likened to Chanel No. 5! At night these pails were replaced with Scottish pin head oatmeal, which took all night to cook for our breakfast the following morning, it really did threaten to put hairs on your chest and produce muscles like dumbbells.

The pantry led off the kitchen where all the washing up took place, no fancy machines, just masses of household soda, and butt ends of soap added to the water, which really did give you chapped red hands. The wall above the sink was lined with antique pine plate racks, and deep cupboards. Leading out of the pantry was the laundry with an old clothes boiler in the corner, and the ceiling covered with racks for drying the laundry. This also had been turned into a milk cooling room (on the instructions of the War Agricultural Committee), where it became Flo's daily job to sterilise all the milking equipment. A strange combination of milk alongside iron saucepans stewing on top of the old clothes boiler containing handkerchiefs and babies' nappies – which ensured that after a good old boiling they would appear whiter than white, just like angel's wings!

Leading out of this room was our artery of life – the air-raid shelter, previously known as the dairy room. It was a wonderful room and I suspect it had been the part used for the inn way back in the pilgrim days, it had that feel about it. Being at the end of the house where the ground rose sharply, it was mainly below ground level. It had a flagstone floor and stone slab shelves all around the room. My father positioned his keg of beer at the far end, and he proudly boasted that it was never allowed to run dry, for he always had a back-up barrel at the ready!

My mother had furnished it with a host of chairs, a carpet and an electric fire. She must have known that many, many hours were going to have to be spent holed up in here during the war years. She had also organised a food cupboard and a gas hob to boil milk and water. Audrey's stretcher bed was designated to one of the stone shelves and the outside walls were heavily protected by sandbags, thus giving us a feeling of security.

Somehow, almost without realising it, we were slipping into our new-found lifestyle. The farm animals were increasing by the week. The chickens proved to be pretty trouble free, for my grandmother was anxious to give a hand for as long as she was able and Nellie, who was so fond of her budgies and canaries, felt that she could soon become attached to chickens, and indeed she did.

The pigs lived in good, strong pig houses. Mucking them out was taken on by Flo as her nursery duties were obviously decreasing as Diana grew older. When our cowman was called up she eventually took on milking the cows as well for we had had a disastrous period when my father hired a temporary cowman. He regularly wrapped himself around a bottle and entered his private world of oblivion, leaving our cows crying out to be milked. My father was home on leave when this crisis arose and he was seen heading for the milking parlour with his three-legged stool and a bucket. Our noses were pressed to the window with curiosity and we didn't have to wait long, we heard the crash of hoof hitting bucket and my father appeared dung spattered, limping, and cursing like mad – without so much as a drop of milk. He was never to be seen entering the milking parlour again. A cow you see is a sensitive lady and likes to be handled with a gentle touch.

Also during his two weeks leave my mother had been grumbling to him that it was high time that he put his MI5 duties to one side and concentrated his attentions on his youngest daughter. 'You're never home Irving, and Diana is missing out on so many little treats, why don't you take her to the open air circus – Bertram Mills has come to Guildford this week, now see what you can do to obtain tickets.' That was a royal command and my father got the message. He toddled off to Guildford, then at lunch announced that he had managed to buy the last two seats on sale. They were the most expensive in the front row, so that meant Diana would have a first class view of everything, he said.

Diana was dressed up in her very best silk smocked dress from Harrods, with its matching blue coat with silk collar and cuffs, her little strapped shoes were red leather, she really did look a picture with her blonde curls. Off they went to the matinée to return home some hours later in a very different state. Apparently, according to my father, the 'big top' was packed to the gunnels, with a great many servicemen in the audience. All had gone well until the lions' cages were erected in the centre of the arena. My father continued, 'In paraded the lions with a tremendous amount of whip cracking on the part of the lion tamer, the audience was hushed with anticipation of what was about to follow. My dears, you should have seen those lions, they gnashed their teeth and swished their tails, and given the chance would have devoured their trainer in an instant. Each lion had a certain trick to perform, and all the while the trainer never once took his commanding eyes off them, until, that is, one particular lion decided he didn't want to do his trick and that's when all bedlam let loose, for he decided to relieve himself, and, can you believe it, a jet with the force of a fire fighter's hose came straight at us, unable as we were to move, we found ourselves drenched in a matter of seconds! The servicemen in the audience thought it was hilarious and part of

the act, and were clapping and cheering to see an officer being del-
uged with lion's urine. The trainer, unaware of the situation, turned
towards the source of the laughter, spotted what was happening and
gave his whip a crack in the direction of the lion, which immediately
had the effect of turning off the tap. But by then it was too late, I'm
afraid Diana's clothes are ruined, my uniform with any luck will
clean, and being the same colour will hopefully not stain.'

Well, my mother hit the roof, and my poor father came under
some very heavy ack ack fire. 'Irving, how could you? Of course you
could have ducked aside, lay on the ground or done something, anything at all – look at Diana's beautiful coat, it will never clean that's
obvious, and what's more it was brand new and pre-war – it will be
impossible to replace. Oh! And what a stink, you both smell like a
public lavatory, you'll have to change in the downstairs cloakroom,
you certainly can't take that smell upstairs.' Diana all the while found
the whole escapade really exciting and kept saying she wanted to be
a lion tamer when she grew up. The clothes were sent with apologies
to the dry cleaners, who returned them with equal apologies saying
that it was impossible to remove the stains!

My father in the meantime had returned to MI5 and had mentioned the whole unfortunate episode to one of the Bertram Mills
brothers, who was also in MI5. He said 'Irving old boy, get your wife
to send your daughter's clothes to our circus cleaners, they can remove
stains from anything, they are used to dealing with situations like that.'
This my mother did, and once again they were returned with the now
familiar note that although every method had been tried, the stains
still remained. The final outcome was a personal letter to my mother
from the circus saying that they would happily replace all items ruined.
With that my mother made a beeline for the most expensive shop in
London – 'The White House', and was able to buy an exquisite silk
smocked dress and coat, in a size larger, almost identical, but twice as
expensive, which was to last Diana for at least two years.

In the early months of the war my mother was delighted with the
way that our increasing animal population had settled in. All, that

is, with the exception of the bullocks. We had plenty of field space for them to charge around in, but our hedges were far from bullock proof and somehow they managed to find every gap – if there wasn't a gap then they'd make one and always in the dead of night, never the daytime. We had a particularly chauvinistic farmer living along-side our farmlands, who took great delight in phoning my mother at all hours of the night saying 'your bullocks are charging past my house up the road, will you please do something about them.' Never once did he volunteer to help her, knowing full well that she was a woman amongst other women at the farm and nursing a sick child.

She and Flo would sling their coats on over their nightdresses, arm themselves with sticks and darkened torches (we had to cover the torch head with two layers of tissue paper) and off they would set in the dead of night to try and find these wretched bullocks down the byways. Two women alone, in the dark, in wartime were so vulner-able. Having found the bullocks, usually munching roadside grass, they would proceed to coax them home again. This would all be related to my father at the War Office, a safe distance away, who really thought it quite amusing. The Guildford police were marvellous and were always eager to help in any way they could. Years later when relating this story it could be seen to be funny, but it was so exhausting at the time.

An amusing and highly embarrassing incident happened, which involved my father and a very dear friend of his by the name of John Roberts. John was a millionaire and my father acted as his solicitor, which in itself proved to be a pretty full-time business, for John had a short fuse and was known from time to time to act on impulse. If, for example, he had problems on the telephone then he would simply tear it out by the roots, with ensuing summonses, which my father would then have to deal with. He was extremely handsome, and six-foot-six in height and could play the most dreamy music on the piano all night long, just so long as he was kept topped up with beers or whiskies. He wasn't very old, which added to his magic charm.

At the beginning of the war he was desperately keen to join the Navy, and it was said by my father that he had remained on the

Admiralty steps for a fortnight until the powers that be became so sick of seeing him that they enrolled him as an AB – an able bodied seaman. Well as you can imagine, he was an absolute wow in the Navy and was posted to the transatlantic run, where he collected friends like other people collect stamps. Upon arriving in New York, he and his Naval rating pals would head off for the high life – all paid for by John.

He had on this occasion come down to spend a night at Warren Farm House. I had been out with a new Naval officer friend, who happened to live just a bit further up our road with his family, his father being an admiral. As we entered the farmhouse I was aware of syncopated music wafting along the passageway leading from our drawing room, and I knew at once who had arrived to liven up the mood. I took my Sub Lieutenant in to meet John and some of his friends who were also staying the night, and before we knew it a party was in the making. 'Have a whisky Richard,' said John, and he poured out a really 'big boy' measure, and before long I saw another and another pass in Richard's direction, and still the music played on. Suddenly we became aware that Richard was no longer with us. 'Where's he gone to?' asked my father, 'To the loo I imagine' John replied, and in our lighthearted mood, almost like playing hide and seek, we went in search of Richard. We finally tracked him down – in the kitchen, curled up like a baby, alongside old Towser on the horsehair one ended sofa. 'Oh for heavens sake', I exclaimed, 'just look at the state he's in, he looks just like an angora rabbit, I'll go in search of a clothes brush.' The poor chap staggered to his feet, full of embarrassment, and obviously alarmed at his appearance, for did I not mention that this old sofa was sacrosanct to Towser?! A naval officer's uniform was made from a special material, melton cloth, it was almost as soft as velvet and, as a result, attracted every hair and bit of fluff within a ten-foot radius. However, finally with the three of us brushing him down we passed him fit to be driven home.

My poor father was filled with remorse at having got this young naval officer into this inebriated state, and felt that he had let the admiral down as one father to another. All John could do was to laugh his head off. We piled into Puffing Billy and set off at a cracking pace with the old car backfiring and spluttering – the Home Guard at the roadblock certainly were well aware that we were heading towards them. We were signalled to stop whereupon we had to show our identity passes, torches were shone into the car and the signal was given for us to proceed. We turned the corner and Richard's house came into view, the boys got out, shook him warmly by the hand, straightened his cap and pointed him in the direction of his gate. We turned around and headed for home, not intending to stop at the road block, for we had only passed through it a few minutes earlier – we shot through it, and I was aware that 'Halt!' had been shouted – 'Carry on Irving' said John. 'The silly bastards must have recognised us from the noise this car is making!' 'BANG', a shot rang out, followed by a booming 'HALT!' Well, that had a sobering effect, so we backed up the car, and allowed them to go through their procedure. To watch my father and his friend made me realise that they were still only schoolboys at heart!

5

LIFE GOES ON

Haymaking was our first arable exercise and after the first sum-mer we really became very good at it. We had the greatest of fun, and I clearly remember the lovely summer weather, not only for haymaking but for harvesting as well, throughout the war years. With the haymaking in full swing I recall the sweet smell of the freshly cut hay. Old Stjarni would be harnessed up to the one and only cart we possessed, and we would be out gathering until the last glints of daylight had disappeared from the sky.

The actual cutting was done by a stooped and wizened old coun-try man called Old Thomas, who used to walk at a steady snail's pace to and from our farm from Chilworth some three miles away. He carried his long scythe over his shoulder and to watch him cut-ting the hay with a lilting, gliding rhythm, moving across the hay meadows was a joy to behold. Those characters are now sadly a thing of bygone days. Surely to be a master of a craft outshone by far the master who accrued worldly goods by his quick wit? Looking back we were such amateurs, but somehow, as a result, madly efficient, and it was the amateurs that, in the main, won the war.

After the haymaking came harvesting, our very first was to follow in August. My father made detailed plans with the Army to let us have eight soldiers on loan to help us gather it in. My job was to go and collect them from the barracks in our ancient, but nonetheless extremely dignified Puffing Billy. This darling car had been bought by my father just before the war as a station car, he would drive it to the station, park it, and then return home in it the same evening. Elegant it may have been in the eyes of the beholder, but quiet – no! It roared like a bull, for the silencer was missing and at times I was told that people were tempted to run for shelter, for the noise made was similar to a Messerschmitt in full action. We were not permitted to use headlights without having proper covers fitted, so as a temporary measure we tied the head lamps up in several thicknesses of yellow dusters, making night driving pretty hazardous, for there were no signposts. We relied on the Good Lord for guidance and white blobs painted on trees, that is, if you could see the trees!

Puffing Billy's duties were very varied to say the least. One of his uses was by my mother three days a week to collect pigswill – with a trailer fitted on the back Flo or the cowman would set off with my mother to empty the special pigswill dustbins left outside peoples gates. The swill consisted of vegetable scraps and potato peelings, and stale bread which had to be saved by law. All this heaving of heavy bins was no job for a lady, but as I have already said my mother never shied away from the job in hand. After collection it had to be cooked up in the galvanized buckets in the kitchen, there were three separate smells all vying with each other to be the strongest – the pigswill, the chickenswill and last, but certainly not least, the dog food – but more about that later.

To return to harvesting, it was arranged that I should report to the barracks to collect our soldiers at eight o'clock in the morning. There they were waiting for me, shirt sleeves rolled up, all bright eyed and bushy tailed and one by one they proceeded to pile into the car. It soon became obvious that not all of them were going to fit into the car on one journey; I would have to make two trips, I decided, for they were big chaps and Puffing Billy although willing, was only small. They told my father that they had all been through Dunkirk and never, but never, had they had such an exciting drive as they'd had with his daughter. I expect I was showing off!

The harvesting took four days and what fun we all had. My father fixed up a barrel of beer in one corner of the field and my mother had cooked a huge leg of ham from one of our very own pigs. This we ate with wartime bread, which, believe it or not, was delicious, it had the natural husks left in it resulting in a marvellous flavour. We made our own butter from the milk taken from Buttercup our Jersey cow, and my aunt in Canada kept us supplied with cheese, what more could one ask for? We all worked like beavers, breaking for our picnic lunch, then carrying on until the sun had tucked herself away beyond the horizon. Then home across the fields to the farmhouse, where Nellie would be waiting with a feast fit for a king – home-grown roast chicken and vegetables, followed by delicious fruit grown in our vegetable garden. The gramophone would be working overtime, and as these evenings passed I never dreamed that I could be so happy, if only, I thought, the harvesting could go on forever.

My sister Audrey, still in hospital, was far from well and the bombing of London was intensifying, which was so worrying for my parents. One morning the telephone rang to say that the children's ward at St Thomas's had been bombed causing some damage, luckily at the end farthest away from my sister. They suggested that as she was so ill they would like to send her home and could we arrange to have a nurse for her, to share the duties with my mother? As a result the house became a hive of activity, for her room had to be prepared, also a room for her nurse, which meant more doubling up than ever. My mother was in her element, she always rose to a challenge, her adrenalin was ticking over at top speed. We waited all day in anticipation of Audrey's arrival in an ambulance, finally the sound of a strange engine was heard approaching and we all dashed out to welcome her home to the bosom of her family once more. My mother announced that from now on she was going to take two hours sleep every afternoon, in order that she could remain up all night, to be thoroughly alert to organise Audrey's move to the shelter from her bedroom on her stretcher should the air-raid warning sound. This she did throughout the whole of the war.

By now I was well on the way to joining the WAAF. It really involved a colossal amount of red tape, endless interviews, followed by medicals, and weeks seemed to drag into months and I had to keep it a deep secret from the family. I suppose I found it frustrating.

During these weeks of waiting I met a delightful Canadian officer called Reg. He was older than I, but with all the charm in the world, he swept me off my feet, or so I liked to think at the time! I had never been organised before and he certainly took charge of my life, every spare second that he had. We rode, we danced, we played tennis and swam. My heart was in a whirl and to be plied with roses or chocolates on each date made me feel just like one of the glamorous film stars that my friend and I used to sit and drool over in the cinema – no wonder he turned my heart. So, imagine my shock when he told me one day that he was married, unhappily. One soon learnt that most married men during the war said that they were unhappily married if they wanted to take out a pretty girl. I felt miserable, for I had always been brought up to believe that marriage meant for life, for better or for worse. My parents would be appalled and I knew that I dare not tell them. Because I was being deceitful, I became sad and guilt-ridden, disliking myself intensely.

But, as fate would have it, or, I like to think, luck perhaps was a better word, my father found out about it and we were summoned to the drawing room one Sunday afternoon. He looked severely grim-faced and I felt like I was at the Old Bailey. Completely ignoring me he lashed into this young officer, with a flow of words the like of which I had never heard before. Was this gentle man, now so enraged, my father? He fixed Reg with a steely stare and in a cold calculated voice he told him that he was in no position to take anybody's daughter out – let alone his! That the war could, and probably would, last for years and in no way during the war and 3,000 miles away from home could he expect to obtain a divorce. Imagine my surprise when he took a Bible from the bookcase and asked us to place our hands upon it and swear never to see each other again. What an undertaking. I was utterly desolate as I watched the, then, love of my life disappear up the drive, gone forever.

This milestone in my life caused me to experience a multitude of confused feelings, anger and embarrassment at being made to feel like a child, which I felt that I certainly was not. I then went to my bedroom and locked the door, flung myself down on my bed and had a really good cry. It is always annoying to have to admit when one is in the wrong, but in this case my father was so right, for he knew what was best for me and could see that I was getting out of my depth. I eventually became grateful to him for disentangling me before I possibly could have burnt my fingers.

Three months later I had fallen in love with an American boy in the RAF flying bombers, called Bill. In love I say, but not the deep-seated love I kept locked up in my heart for Donald, who was by now far away from home, heaven knows where. I have a little laugh to myself when I think that today the young would think that I was crazy to have obeyed my father, but obey we did in those far away days, really with no long-lasting malice or grudge. That was no doubt the reason for united family life, the head of one's family, one's father, was the linchpin. He would make the decisions and his family by and large would abide by them, and as a result we all felt incredibly secure.

Although Warren Farm House was bulging at the seams, my father's bedroom was sacrosanct and despite the fact that his Army career in MI5 meant that he was away from home most of the war, my mother always kept his room ready, just in case he was given a few days leave. But in between his rare visits she would allow his room to be used to accommodate 'her Canadian boys', who might find themselves with a leave pass, and nowhere to go.

On one such occasion a captain and his driver arrived on her doorstep. His driver was called Tiny, but there was nothing very tiny about him, as he was six feet and seven inches tall. My mother decided to put him in my father's bedroom, which was furnished with lovely antique furniture and a very substantial bed which had a large horsehair mattress that weighed a ton! This room, for our friend Tiny, proved to be an assault course. Not only was the ceiling very low and heavily oak beamed, on which he managed to crack his head every time he got out of bed, but there was also a step down to the lower end of the room, which he didn't see, causing him to end up in an undignified heap. Whether it was this series of mishaps, or just a very weak bladder, he managed to soak my father's bed, causing it to smell like the public lavatories on Paddington station! Nellie discovered it before anyone else, because being deaf she had developed a very strong sense of smell, which led her to my father's bed. She rushed to find my mother with the devastating news, 'Oh, Madam, the Master's bed is soaked through to the floor, what are we going to do, he's coming home tonight isn't he?'

My mother went to inspect the damage and immediately rounded up all the able bodied amongst us. We had, she said, 'to manoeuvre it down the stairs, we'll get it round the corner somehow, it will be difficult but we'll just have to face that problem when we come to it.' Well, what a pantomime, Laurel and Hardy would have given their back teeth to have been able to use a scene such as this. The mattress was impossibly heavy, cumbersome and totally unbending. My mother and Flo were at one end of it, Mrs Bill, our cowman's wife, and Nellie at the other, and I was to manipulate in the middle. What my mother hadn't taken into consideration when planning her campaign was that both Mrs Bill and Nellie had pretty colossal busts and as we twisted, pushed and squeezed this wretched mattress around the right-angled turn in the stairs, both busty ladies got themselves firmly wedged between the mattress and the wall and in muffled voices were plaintively calling for help. 'Oh do be quiet you two, we've got to get this mattress downstairs and out into the garden to wash and dry it and don't forget girls, we've got to then get it back upstairs again before the Major returns home this evening. Wiggle anyway you can and push now – push!' There were so many 'ows' and 'ouches' and grunts and puffs, and miracle of miracles with an enormous push from me in the middle we all ended up in a tousled heap at the bottom of the stairs, with the heavy mattress stinking to high heaven on top of us.

With all the noise we were making my grandmother and Aunt Lilah had come to see what on earth was going on. The total look of amazement on their faces caused my mother to tell them that moths had got into the mattress and she wanted to leave it outside in the sun to get rid of them. This seemed to satisfy their curiosity and they toddled off back to my grandmother's wing of the house.

Little did I realise that my destiny was signed and sealed the day that my mother received a letter from her sister in Canada, to tell her that her friend's nephew had come over to England to join the RAF so she was writing to ask my mother to offer him hospitality. The Battle of Britain was at its full horrific height and little did I realise that this Canadian boy, whom I was later to marry, was up there in those clear summer blue skies fighting for his very existence. My mother asked me to write to invite him to the farm, which quite frankly at the time I found to be a bit tiresome, and in turn we had a letter in reply thanking us politely, but he doubted that he would be in our part of the world, so that was that, we had done our duty, and he in turn had done his!

However, upon his return to Canada in 1942 on a course, he was told off in no uncertain terms by his aunt for not following up our kind invitation. He apparently promised her that he would put the matter right on his return to England. An awful lot of water had passed beneath the bridge since the initial invitation was issued in the early part of the war. He had become engaged to a Canadian girl from Ottawa and I had joined the WAAF and was not exactly sitting in the barracks pining my heart out or twiddling my thumbs with loneliness!

Warren Farm House was a haven of idyllic peacefulness, tucked away in the folds of a valley with our fields lying all around it. At times it was hard to imagine that there was a war going on – but going on it was, and little did we realise on that glorious day that our home, within a few hours, was to be on the front line.

Our immediate neighbours, although some distance away, were spinster sisters, who were quite delightfully charming, of the lavender and lace era, graciousness and dignified charm. They took great interest in the Gane girls, as indeed we did in them. They, like everyone else who had a large house, had to take in evacuees and they had a mother and her two children billeted on them. They came from the bomb-torn East End of London. Their father was a docker, the very salt of the British earth. They didn't take particularly kindly to the English countryside; it was a whole strange new world for them and living in a rather grand house no doubt made them feel ill at ease, despite the kindness of the two spinsters. The children were homesick for Bermondsey and their father. Their mother was missing her husband, who would try and come and visit his little family whenever he could get away from his job and his nightly fire watching duties around the London docks area. The poor chap was not allowed to stay overnight in the ladies' house, the thought of a man staying there was unheard of, so it fell to my mother to find him a bed in our house, I think it was a camp bed hastily assembled in our morning room. Heaven knows what the ladies thought might happen to them, he was such a nice chap too.

The pattern of their brief meetings was always the same, he would take his wife to the pictures, followed by a drink in the pub before their slow walk home – I say slow because we had fields of waving corn and a large warm cosy barn and they were able on these all too rare occasions to get to know one another again as married people do. Being of a romantic nature, I liked to think that these scenarios were far, far better than a cramped little bedroom in a semi in the heart of London's bombed out dockland.

On one such night the husband had returned to our farmhouse, had enjoyed the proverbial cup of tea in the kitchen with all of us, chewing the fat and discussing the war news. Nellie had covered her budgies with their night curtain, taken the swill buckets off the stove so that they could cool overnight and had replaced them on the gas ring with the saucepan of porridge, to be cooked all night and served at breakfast in the morning. The dogs had selected their own special niches to settle down for the night, with our ever special Pluto taken out to his kennel underneath the chestnut tree, to stand guard overnight. He really was our knight in shining armour. The time had come to climb the stairs to bed, but as we reached the top stair we suddenly became aware of a tremendous rushing noise, as though a hurricane was about to demolish the house. As it passed over us the old house started to sway crazily and was almost lifted off its very foundations with this evil wind. This was quickly followed by a vast explosion, which had the whole house shaking and shuddering as if it were having an epileptic fit – what on earth was it?

We froze to the spot in fright. My parents were blown out of the bathroom such was the blast – my mother had been attending to a particularly painful blister that my father had on his heel and what a sight they made! Despite our fear of the unknown one could only collapse in uncontrollable laughter to see my father in his baggy kneelength vyella underpants and his sleeved vest, trying to pick himself up off the floor with some degree of dignity.

My mother was first to collect herself, she grabbed her dressing gown and was then ready for action. The poor little man from London gave way to panic, he kept on repeating over and over again that in the morning he was going back to London and taking his family with him. 'In London' he said, 'at least we have ack ack guns to shoot the bastards down, but here all you get are the bloody bombs, and the sound of the German planes – why, you can't ever hear those in London, because we have the guns you see.' Nobody was really paying attention to him, we were all too busy with our own private fears.

My grandmother and Aunt Lilah had now appeared on the scene, obviously petrified. Before we knew it there was pandemonium reigning, with everyone trying to talk at the same time. 'Now mother,' said my father, 'there is nothing to get alarmed about, the house is still standing so I suggest you take Lilah back to your bedroom and I will keep you informed just as soon as I can throw some clothes on and go and find out what has happened.'

Nellie then appeared in her hair curlers and voluminous nightgown, quite oblivious of the vast explosion. By this time all our evacuees and family were assembled in the upstairs hallway when there was a loud banging on our front door. As always, my mother had assumed the role of general and was first to open the door, to be faced once again by a group of the Home Guard, but on this occasion fronted by their captain. 'We have bad news for you I'm afraid' the captain said, 'there has been a "dog fight" over Guildford and the German has off-loaded his bombs to make a quick get away. We have reason to believe that apart from the big one that has already exploded, the rest of them have also landed in your garden and surrounding fields.'

My father, still in his vest and baggy underpants, had joined my mother at the door and was in rather a flap to put it mildly – concerned for his family. 'My dear Monty' he said, 'I want you to round everybody up and pile them into the car and leave here immediately – I don't care where you go, but go immediately – you must.' He was hopping about from foot to foot whilst he was pleading with her – his underpants by now at half mast! Despite the seriousness of the situation, once again to see my normally dignified father looking this way reduced us all to uncontrollable laughter bordering on hysterics.

Despite my father's pleading, my mother was quite adamant, 'No, Irving, if we are to be blown up, then we will be blown up here at Warren Farm House, for no way am I going to risk bundling Audrey into the car in the dead of night – the idea is sheer lunacy and would probably kill her.' It was obvious that she would refuse to budge.

By this time the cowman Bill with his wife, his four year old, and ten-month-old baby daughter had come rushing over from their little cottage on the other side of the farmyard along with more officials, in the form of Air-Raid Wardens. This was a new experience for them and as they spoke at top speed it was obvious that they too were frightened. They repeated pretty much the same message that had been given to us by the Home Guard.

Yes, the bombs were on our land and on inspection of the garden a huge hole had been spotted in a flowerbed, this they feared could be an unexploded bomb, or possibly a time bomb. This, of course, caused a whole new panic, if there was more than one time bomb, then the house could be blown to pieces willy nilly.

My mother had taken complete control. 'Now Irving' she said, 'I want you to round up everyone and settle them in the shelter, Flo will put the kettle on and I suggest you all have a cup of tea. I am going out with Bill and a couple of torches and we will have a thorough search everywhere, and see what we can discover.' My father wanted to object, but she didn't give him the time, for like 'willow the wisp' in her old mac and wellies she and Bill disappeared out into the night, and all we could do was to sit and wait in the shelter, where we spent the entire night.

What a strange collection of human beings we were, of all ages and sizes. My grandmother and a surly looking Aunt Lilah; my father, who was obviously demented with worry about my mother's whereabouts and the risk of exploding bombs; dear, deaf old Nellie wanting a minute by minute account; the evacuees – the colonel and his lady, the medical student, the little man from London who was worrying about his family next door, but not daring to go and look for them, and the docker's children Helen and John showing no fear whatsoever, the same could be said for Diana. Audrey lay on her stretcher bed, never complaining, with her nurse who was holding her hand. Flo was brewing the tea and Mrs Bill was sitting in the corner chair cuddling her two children. Mrs Bill, as she always did on these stressful occasions, would unbutton her blouse and expose one large breast which she would offer first to the baby and then to the four year old – age didn't come into the reckoning. It was for bairns an age-old comforter. It was an incredible scene which at first used to make me very embarrassed, especially when we had visitors and Canadian soldiers staying, but somehow, as the war wore on it became a part of our wartime scenario.

As soon as dawn broke the activity became immense. The Army had discovered five more bombs, two in the garden, and three in our fields – all time bombs. Those in the garden were luckily at the far end and well away from the house. They exploded in their own time at twenty-minute intervals and little damage was done, apart from making more gaps in the hedges for our bullocks to escape through!

The house and garden were shrouded in white chalk dust, it seemed that snow had come to the farm in September. The huge hole in the flower bed, that had caused all the fuss in the first place, turned out not to actually be a bomb, but only a large section of bomb casing which had landed in the flower bed when the initial big bomb had exploded. It really was a miracle that not one iota of damage was suffered by our house.

The whole town it seemed flocked to see the enormous bomb crater in the middle of one of our fields. It was a one thousand pounder and the windows in many houses that surrounded our land had been blown out, with shattered glass lying everywhere. The strange thing was that none of our animals, the cows, horses and bullocks who were grazing in the fields, suffered any ill effects from the gigantic explosion. A year or so later, we arranged with the prisoner of war camp on Merrow Downs for them to send us a few trusted prisoners to come and fill in the crater, but the landmark always remained. At the time, however, we felt quite smug at seeing German prisoners having to put right some of their own dirty work!

I have always felt that we should have put up some sort of plaque to record this terrifying incident that occurred on our peaceful land – for the war had come with a vengeance to Warren Farm House.

6

A GROWING
HOUSEHOLD

Dear old Warren Farm House was by now bursting at the seams. There just seemed to be no end to the comings and goings; just how Nellie and my mother managed to produce enough food for everyone, day in and day out, was beyond comprehension.

A Land Army girl was the latest addition to the household, a super girl from Lancashire called Enid. This took a great workload from Flo, who was then able to help Nellie with all the food preparation. I seem to remember her either peeling mountains of potatoes or grumbling like mad at stripping peas and, as she would say, 'Beastly blackcurrants'. But how lucky we were to have all our own produce in the garden and on the farm. For example, we had huge bowls of strawberries, raspberries, gooseberries and the afore-mentioned 'beastly' black and redcurrants, piles of rhubarb, and from the greenhouse there was a constant supply of black grapes, peaches and nectarines. There was asparagus in the vegetable garden, our orchard was stocked with apple, pear, plum and damson trees and my mother used to pickle walnuts from the old walnut tree. As fortune would have it my father managed to retain our pre-war gardener; slow he may have been and wracked with arthritis, but he never shirked his duties and was a treasure. Our meadows were full of field mushrooms and each morning at break of day we would dash out to gather them – some of them were so large they were the size of breakfast plates!

Canadians were by now arriving in greater numbers as news of us spread amongst their barracks – as did the gifts of food, chocolate bars and clothing coupons which they gave to my mother. By foregoing our bacon rations we were allowed to keep a side of our pig, which not only gave us bacon, but chops, a leg and two juicy trotters which are so delicious when cooked and pressed into a bowl and eaten cold. The cheek of the pig could also be treated in the same manner; my mouth is watering just thinking about it after all these years. Paupers we may have been in some ways, but we ate like kings.

I must also refer to our chickens, and their huge dark brown eggs, the flavour of which, like the pig, I can remember to this day. They had the full run of a field and the farmyard, it was lovely to see them scratching about and making happy contented chicken noises. We had a very special little bantam hen called 'Banty' who was such a character – she loved to sit on a clutch of eggs, she wasn't fussy – one time it could be ducks, but she had a special attraction for turkey eggs. She would proudly stalk around the farmyard, clucking and chastising them, as each day they would be getting larger and larger, and eventually she would be forced to twist her neck, looking up towards the sky in order to see them with her bright little eyes. She would take no nonsense from them, she lived to a ripe old age and we loved her. She reared a mallard duck whom we called 'quack-quack', he had the most beautiful colourings and orange galoshes on his feet. The two of them were inseparable until, sadly a fox put a sudden end to Banty's friend. Our turkeys demanded a lot of care in their early days as they were very delicate to rear. I remember helping my mother to chop up stinging nettles very finely which she would then mix up with hard boiled eggs; this would be their daily diet until they became hardy.

With so many people in our house it meant that the meat ration coupons enabled us to have a good roast from time to time. My heart always went out to people, especially the elderly living on their own, for them it meant a meagre chop or piece of stewing steak the size of a packet of cigarettes. I know that my mother had a collection of old dears whom she used to call on and give them special treats from time to time.

My mother by this time was heavily involved with her wheeler dealing. She had a good thing going with one of our neighbours, who lived with his family in an imposing house at the back of our fields in Longdown. He was anxious to go shares with our pigs, saying to my mother that he could lay his hands on macaroni sweepings from a factory floor, and if he could keep her in macaroni, could he have a half quota of pig? It seemed an excellent idea, so they shook hands on the deal.

My father on the other hand obviously felt that he was being kept in the dark about something and how right were his suspicions. But had he not made it perfectly plain that in no way was his family to get involved in any form of black marketeering? Because of this ultimatum my mother had no intention of involving him, subsequently he showed his displeasure with the odd comment to my mother, 'that man always seems to be in our house, why is he here my dear?' My mother when challenged would always rub her hands together and light up another cigarette, and so the subject was dropped.

On a particularly foul and storm ridden winter's night there was urgent banging on the laundry room door. Nellie answered it, and then hastily came to find my mother, 'Oh madam,' she said, 'do come quickly, there seems to be a man at the door in a state of high doh, he says he must see you at once.' Well we had all learnt never to question my mother at times like this! The stranger told her that he had been up to our neighbour with a dead pig in his van but he could get no answer when he knocked at the door. As he had been given our address previously by our neighbour he was throwing himself on my mother's mercy. 'I can't take this carcass home ma'am, it's too risky having to go through all the road blocks and all – you'll just have to take it and that's all there is to it.' Well, my mother was rubbing her hands and puffing like mad on her cigarette, for the thought of handling a full-sized dead pig was a major problem. There was never any doubt that she would handle it though – just think of all the lovely pork she could serve up to her enormous wartime family. 'All right, I'll take it, but you will have to hide it out of sight in a safe place for me.' The man followed her out into the dark on this stormy and unfriendly night and she got him to stow it away in an unused hen house, under a good layer of straw. I have never to this day been told how she managed to butcher it, but I expect that Fred our fish-monger came to her rescue, no doubt for a share in this porker. All I know is that he seemed to be paying a lot of visits to the farm. My father on the other hand kept announcing, rather like a gramophone record stuck in a groove, 'How marvellous this pork is my dear, obvi-ously the butcher must have had a large consignment, for we seem to be having pork more often than anything else!' My mother never batted an eyelid – and neither did we!

My mother cultivated her butcher, fishmonger, grocer and wine merchant – I'm not sure in what order, for we never dared to enquire! In fact we had to pretend not to know anything about her little trips to town. She would be seen toddling up the drive with a purpose, with a large shopping basket covered by a clean tea cloth, full to overflowing with acceptable goodies ranging from large deep brown eggs, butter or a fat chicken, or even some of the gifts that the Canadian boys had brought her – like dried fruit or chocolate bars.

My father, being a solicitor, had drummed it into us on the very day that war was declared that he would not tolerate any member of his family meddling in the black market. We all, he said, had to manage like everyone else and too bad if we went short. I must say that I couldn't but help notice my mother after that statement – she had a naughty twinkle in her eye and she obviously had no intention of keeping to that high moral code. Her philosophy in time of war was that fair exchange was no robbery. If she could give someone a dozen eggs, a pound of home cured bacon, even a chicken or a duck, then it was quite acceptable that they in return would give her a bottle of whisky, a roast of pork, a pure silk nightie – minus coupons – or some unobtainable make-up for me!

The system worked wonderfully well, with only the odd hiccough. One such occasion was when she called me and said 'Muriel, I want you to go and see our grocer and ask him for 56lb of preserving sugar, I want to make strawberry jam this afternoon.' She failed to warn me that I was to ask him in privacy because our ration at that particular time was a mere few ounces. Off I went and waited in his crowded shop where he eventually appeared from the back, on spotting me he said, 'Hello, and what can I get for you today?' I smiled back and said, 'My mother wants 56lb of sugar to make strawberry jam.' The shop fell silent, and I realised that I had obviously put both my feet in it, especially when the good man replied, 'Impossible, will you tell your mother that we happen to be in the middle of a war, she must keep to her allotted ration.' I nearly died of embarrassment and slunk off towards the car. The little man came out of his shop in great confusion, for it was a known fact that my mother's account there amounted to a pretty hefty chunk of his monthly profit, she did after all smoke sixty cigarettes a day – Craven A – all purchased from his shop. Full of twitches and nervous spluttering he told me to drive the car around to the back of the shop. 'Of course she can have the sugar, she usually comes herself when she wants a particularly large quantity of anything' he said. My reply to him was, 'Well, she said she will see you right with this and that when she calls tomorrow she will bring you the six chickens you asked her for.' Incidentally, this upright pillar of society was the mayor – and a truly wonderful fellow!

Talking of coupons, we also had to have them to purchase petrol, we were allotted so many per month, to use in a specific zone for essential journeys, certainly not for joy riding. It was always interesting to see my mother's return from her trip to town, as her basket would usually be just as bulging as when she set out. This time it would be filled with commodities of another nature or if it wasn't bulging then we knew her purse would be full of coupons for petrol or clothes, or maybe even both!

Her reasoning was far from sinister, she simply wanted to take the best care that she could of her very large wartime family, which was increasing it seemed by the day. She certainly never intended telling my father and he seemingly never guessed what she was up to, or if he did then he certainly never 'let on'. He enjoyed to the full all the spoils of war and would tell her over and over again just how clever she was to provide such delights. She would always smile that wicked smile of hers and we girls knew just what she was thinking!

She had 'tamed' a flying squad policeman who apparently (indeed luckily) fancied me and was only too anxious to help us in any small way so long as he could come to the farm when I was home on leave. He would love to be invited to tea in the farmhouse kitchen, or under the spreading elm trees in our beautiful back garden in the summer time. He was a super chap, we all had a crush on him, even old Nellie and he was so handsome, especially in his uniform. We looked after him in the way of produce and it seemed that whatever I wanted he could lay his hands on; in return for which I would give him a kiss and a big smile. He was indeed a power of strength to my mother when she needed help on the farm, nothing was ever too much trouble. Mysteriously drums of petrol would suddenly appear hidden in our hedgerow from time to time, no questions were asked and we were never absolutely certain which of my mother's friends had left them there!

Our cowman Bill was eventually called up, he was drafted to the Surrey War Agricultural Committee, a total disaster for us so far as the farm was concerned. However, he continued to live in his cottage, for his job was to deliver potatoes to the Army camps in Aldershot. My mother now had the added responsibility of keeping an eye on his wife and young children and by way of gratitude Bill looked after us with petrol and 'this and that'. It was the 'this and that', that helped when caring for the Canadian soldiers as well as all the many other people, in, on and around the farm.

I used to bring my WAAF girlfriends home and of course there was a constant flow of my boyfriends and pre-war friends who were back home on leave. In fact it was a never ending procession passing through the farmhouse, with my mother always there to give a personal welcome.

The winter of 1941 was a harsh one and coal was pretty impossible to get hold of. My mother managed one day to chat a post office engineer into getting her some old telephone poles, no doubt in exchange for some of the goodies in her basket. She paid a shilling per pole. She was able to obtain about a dozen, which were dumped, as many mysterious things were, just inside the by now famous hedgerow. They were far too heavy to be moved. 'Nellie' said my mother in her commander's voice, 'after my rest this afternoon you and I are going up the field to saw up the telephone poles. I have been sorting out a saw for us to use, it will have to be a double-handled one, I know the wood is as hard as rock, but once we get the knack we'll soon have them all sawn up.' Nellie looked aghast and said, 'But how on earth are we going to do it madam, we haven't got a bench up there, and they are too heavy to lift in any case.' 'Nonsense Nellie,' said my mother, 'we don't need a bench, we will lie on our stomachs and manhandle the saw backwards and forwards, don't put obstacles in the way until we get to them,' and that seemed to be the end of the matter.

What a sight they made, one each end of a long two-handled saw with the pole between them, pulling the saw this way and that, with the teeth of the saw getting jammed in the hard wood. With a mammoth amount of grit and determination they finally cut up three poles – which took one whole month. The remaining nine poles were cut up by two Canadian servicemen, who just happened to be in the forestry division and who were working in the Scottish forests. And guess what? It took them two hours!

No one grumbled about the cold when the inglenook fires belted out warm glowing heat from those dry hard logs – they took a very long time to burn away. It was one of the best buys she ever made in wartime.

As I have mentioned, my mother was fearless in our eyes, so imagine my surprise when one afternoon she came rushing into the house in quite a tizzy. We had been aware that the air-raid warning siren had sounded but thought nothing of it, for it was always sounding and one tended to become a little blasé about it. Apparently she was up on the hill feeding the chickens when she became aware of a low flying aircraft circling overhead. Imagining it to be one of our RAF boys she looked up and began waving enthusiastically at it – but was horror struck to find it was actually a German bomber and the crew had seen her waving and had begun to wave back. Her instinct was to stop waving, but a little voice inside her told her to carry on and let them believe that she was probably a German sympathiser. How wise she was, for at that time they had been known to machine gun civilians going about their business on the ground. As soon as the plane passed out of sight, they dropped their deadly parcel on a railway bridge a mile or so away. I was glad to see that she had a human weakness – even if she only showed it on that one occasion.

7

GIRL IN BLUE

I was at this time stationed in the WAAF at Fighter Command Headquarters at Stanmore in Middlesex and my visits home, although brief, were pretty regular. I would dash home with a case full of shirts to be washed. There were no washing machines then, but Flo was marvellous, she would rub and scrub and soon they would be out on the clothes line blowing in the wind. My mother, who prided herself on her ironing ability, would have them ironed and folded all ready to be put back in my case ready for the off once again.

When one has a little problem one's instinct is to rush home to the bosom of the family and let it all pour out. Such had been my week, I had felt like creeping into the ground to be swallowed up, and I so wanted to tell my parents all about it. I had been selected in the WAAF for Special Duties. As the title suggests, it was special and also top secret, so we had to sign on oath the Official Secrets Act. At the time we received a lecture that girls chosen for this particular job were never, never to discuss their work with their parents, their husbands or boyfriends – not *ever* to anyone, anywhere, or it would mean instant discharge with ignominy. This above all really made the job doubly exciting, so imagine my surprise when one day whilst on Watch I was told to report to the Air Chief Marshal and his staff in the main building. It was an awesome meeting and I was quizzed about my movements. Had I, they asked me, talked to anyone about my job? I was near to tears and really petrified, I couldn't throw any light on their concerns, I went back to the Operations Room only to be told that I could not enter, but would have to work in the canteen for the time being. I felt like a criminal – and I didn't for the life of me know why. Everyone looked at me with suspicion and asked continually what had I done? This continued for a further two days, then I was sent for once again. This time I felt certain I would be sent to The Tower of London, no less. Imagine my utter delight, therefore, to be told by the Air Chief Marshal that they owed me an enormous apology. Apparently when my papers were being screened for this Special Duties job, some clerk had put two red crosses beside my name, intending to write an appendix saying that my father was an officer in MI5. The papers had slipped through and it was assumed that the red crosses were an alert of some kind. I felt ten feet tall, but I was told that I couldn't mention this meeting to anyone, so I had to face up to all my friends on Watch, and was unable to explain to them why I had been removed from the Ops Room.

One soon learns that a scandal is only a ten-day wonder, quickly forgotten, and so it was with me. Nevertheless, I wanted to pour out my troubles to my parents, but of course I couldn't. I had unexpectedly been given a twenty-four-hour leave pass and I headed home at top speed. It was a glorious summer's day and the thought of dashing home to spend a few hours away from the hectic pressures in the Ops Room, to be able to soak in a deep hot bath and smooth all my cares away, to don my riding clothes and head off on Sally to visit my favourite haunts, was almost too good to be true, I could hardly wait.

My friend Liz and I travelled together from Stanmore to London on the earliest tube, as she was planning on spending a few precious hours with her family. The scene that greeted us when the tube finally arrived at Waterloo was always the same. The station platforms had become home from home for hundreds of Londoners, who each night would take up residence – mum, dad, gran, the endless kids, dogs, cats, and in cages budgies and canaries. It was a haven of safety, for their own houses, if they hadn't already been bombed, could very well be on that particular night. Their spirits always seemed high, or perhaps, like my mother, they had the happy knack of hiding their feelings at an all time low. Such was the indomitable character of a true Londoner and I always felt that I wanted to make sure that future generations were aware of their tenacious courage in times of adversity. There they would be, with all their bedding in a long row just like a school dormitory, with a canteen set up at one end of the platform and they would go about things just as if they were at home – even to cutting toenails, or bathing the baby! Life had to go on, war or no war was their motto. We picked our way carefully amongst them, with lots of cockney banter, we'd say goodbye and then head off for our respective homes.

I loved my early morning walk up Warren Road, I felt I had beaten the dawning of a new day. All would be quiet, except for the singing of the many birds and the odd dog taking his morning constitutional. I would be almost running as I turned in to our long drive, which coursed its sloping way down to our farmhouse which was tucked well out of sight in the valley. Meadows lay on either side of the drive and in June they were a myriad of wild flowers, nodding their welcome at my homecoming. Sally, my mare and my best friend munched the lush grass, as I approached I called out her name, and then again. At first she did not respond, as though she feared that she was imagining my calling. I called her again, and in a flash she lifted her head and with an ecstatic whinny she galloped full steam ahead in my direction. How foolish we were. 'Sal darling,' I said as I threw my arms around her neck. 'Oh! How I've missed you girl.' She whinnied and I like to think that she was answering me. We stayed like that with me caressing her head and I'm ashamed to say warm tears were trickling down my cheeks. Yes, I really missed my horse so much and all the happy times we had shared together – it was at times such as this that I hated the war, and all the misery it brought.

It was then that I noticed dear old Pluto coming slowly up the drive to greet me with his long tail wagging – yes, it was good to be home – and then Diana appeared carrying a bucket of food for Sally. I was devoted to my baby sister and my admiration for her knew no bounds. She, poor darling, had been propelled into growing up at such an unnatural speed thanks to Adolph Hitler – so many farm chores fell on her young shoulders, but she seemed to accept this as a matter of course.

The main purpose of my leave pass was to make a cake for a delightful French girl on my Watch who was getting married. It was a very romantic story. She had escaped from France to England as soon as France had capitulated, and had joined the WAAF. She too was on Special Duties and had become one of our Watch's most experienced plotters – hooked into Dover, which happened to be the busiest position on the vast grid map. Sometimes during heavy battles in the sky it was impossible for the girl on Dover to change Watch, such was the intensity of her plotting. In quieter moments she had found the time to chat to the RAF sergeant down on the Dover station, one thing led to another and he asked her to marry him.

She had no civilian clothes, so a number of us offered to bring her clothes from our homes and I told her I'd bring a cake for the wedding. Nellie's cakes were famous and I knew that she would oblige. I planned to take a large bowl of strawberries and thick rich cream for her small reception at our billets on the Monday. I only had one slight problem to surmount and that was how I was going to be able to transport it all back to our billet! There was a simple answer, but I had misgivings about whether my mother would agree with me, so I bided my time until I thought the moment was right. 'Mother, I want to ask a small favour.' 'Yes, darling what is it?' she asked. 'Well, I have to get all this clobber and the cake back to camp, and I wondered if you would let me take Puffing Billy? I know you need it on Monday morning to collect the pigswill, but when I come off watch at 5 a.m. I can drive straight home and be back here by 9 a.m. I promise. The wedding isn't until the afternoon, so I can easily get back to camp in good time for that.' There was a pregnant pause whilst my mother tossed the idea around in her mind. 'Well, darling, it sounds simple enough, but although I don't want to appear to be a damp squib, I feel it is far too risky, for I simply have to have the car to collect the pigswill, we have no other form of transport as you know.'

Well, I cajoled her in every possible way I knew how, and finally she agreed, though reluctantly, and I set off in the afternoon with Puffing Billy packed to the gunnels. There were armfuls of flowers from the garden, the white iced wedding cake, and some summer clothes for her trousseau. I was driving along Gunnersbury Avenue without a care in the world when Puffing Billy suddenly began to make the most appalling noise from somewhere underneath. This was all I needed, the noises he made normally were bad enough without this. Being a Sunday everywhere was closed tighter than a clam and at all costs I just had to get back for my Watch at 1 a.m. Eventually I became aware that a police car was hot on my heels flashing it's lights and signalling me to pull into the side. Usually I could win the day, but not with these two. They told me that there was no way I could possibly continue along this residential road making this noise, they had an expert look underneath, suggested that it was something serious, gave me a wicked wink and departed! Charming, I thought, I must be losing my touch.

I continued along at a snail's pace, finally grinding to a stop. Now what? I was really at a loss to know what to do next but, as luck would have it, out of nowhere came a cheery little man, ready and only too willing to be of help. He said that his house was behind me and he would get his neighbour to come and help push the car into his driveway, for he felt that the fault could be serious if the noise was anything to go by. The thought that Puffing Billy could be laid low here for weeks whilst spare parts were found for him appalled me – what on earth would my mother say? He told me that he would call into the garage on his way to London the next morning to get them to come and collect it. I told him of my plight, of how I needed to get to my Headquarters to go on Watch, and also how important it was for my mother to have the car repaired so that she could collect the pigswill – tomorrow was the deadline. He could see that I was in a state. 'Don't you worry my dear, I will flag down a car and ask them to take you back to your Headquarters, it is after all an emergency.' All the cars seemed to be going in the opposite direction, but if nothing else he was determined and he managed to stop a car, the driver of which was willing to turn around and take me back to Stanmore. They were taking their granny home and the car was packed with the family, so it was a very tight squeeze to get me in with all my paraphernalia. In all it was quite an achievement, petrol being rationed meant that people could only travel on a very limited scale and in the case of this particular family it was issued to transport Granny to and fro. Luckily this could be regarded as an emergency.

They were a charming family and only too willing to help. We were laughing and chatting when suddenly a great belch of smoke started to seep out from beneath the bonnet. In great haste we came to a halt and piled out lock stock and barrel onto the pavement, to watched in horror as the smoke became worse. Soon help was at hand, for them at least, as we had fortunately stopped right outside a pub and a taxi was called to transport them home – in the original direction. It didn't help me one little bit as I stood there like orphan Annie with all my goods and chattels stacked around my feet. But you have to be lucky sometimes and my luck was in for at that very moment that a lady staggered out of the public house leaning heavily on her son for support. I ran up to them and related my plight. 'Oh, you poor love,' exclaimed the lady, 'Mike we must drive her back to her station,' she said with several hiccoughs. 'Mother,' was his reply 'we can't, it's the wrong direction for a start and we're short of petrol.' His mother would have none of it, 'Rubbish, I've got some coupons in my bag, we'll be alright.' Well, what a bit of luck, in we piled – along with the cake, the clothes, the flowers and strawberries and cream and set off at a cracking pace with her son looking like a thunder cloud. This time I actually managed to complete the whole journey and arrived with plenty of time to spare to hand all the things over to my French colleague.

I then had to pluck up the courage to telephone my mother and break the bad news about the car. As you can imagine she nearly had fifty fits. But there was absolutely nothing we could do about it and I promised most faithfully that I would get back to the garage and hopefully home just as soon as I could.

I must admit that my concentration was none too accurate on Watch that night, and I was also suffering from severe lack of sleep for I had arisen from my bed twenty-four hours ago and had to face a second night Watch and whatever tomorrow would bring. It's amazing what one can do when one is young. It was obvious that I was going to miss out on the wedding, so I kissed the bride to be and wished her luck as we came off Watch. My friend Liz insisted coming with me for company's sake, as there were no trains running at that early hour we decided to try our hand at hitch-hiking. We were lucky, managing to get a couple of short hitches – at least going in the right direction. Our third attempt was on a vegetable van coming back from Covent Garden. This was to prove pretty hair-raising to say the least. He was a friendly enough bloke, but something must have tickled his hormones and in an instant his whole mood changed and it became very obvious what he was after. It was obvious too that we had to make a quick exit and this is exactly what we did at the next set of traffic lights – much to his surprise and chagrin he didn't get the tasty crumpets for his breakfast after all! The last three miles we tackled on foot at a brisk pace, it was safer by far and after that experience I never hitch-hiked again!

As we approached the house where I had left Puffing Billy, it became obvious that trouble had befallen the area during the night. There were houses with their roofs blown off and glass littered the pavements and front gardens everywhere. Odd houses here and there were smouldering sadly. We stopped someone to ask what had happened and were told that a large land mine had been dropped during the night. I nearly died – my dear Puffing Billy! Had he too gone up in smoke I wondered? Certainly the gentleman's house looked a sorry sight, I just hoped that the two friendly little people who lived there had not been harmed in any way. We knocked on the door and a rather weary looking little lady opened it. She said that they had had a dreadful night. I patiently waited for her to tell me her full story as I did not wish to appear callous, but I longed to have news about the car – I was worried stiff, so after a polite pause I asked her if she could tell me about the car. 'Oh that's all right dear,' she said 'the windows were blown in, or should I say out, on one side, but the windscreen was all right. My husband called at the garage, and they came and collected it about an hour ago.' The feeling of relief was immense and I thanked her warmly as we bade her farewell.

When we reached the garage they were just putting the finishing touches to Puffing Billy as they had apparently had the necessary spare parts in stock. For the large sum of eleven pounds ten shillings we set of happily for Warren Farm House – and the pigswill! Even the broken windows had been replaced – we were elated and so was my mother. She had organised one of her many pals, this time one of our local taxi drivers, to take her on the pigswill round, no doubt in exchange for some goodies out of her basket – for she never thought we would make it. We spent a super day at home and were able to grab a snooze under the elm trees in the afternoon sun, recharging our batteries in readiness for the long journey back to camp to go on Watch at 1 a.m. but this time it was with a light-hearted step – such was life.

8

NEW BEGINNINGS

My sister Audrey by this time was making a miraculous recovery from her long and severe illness. It was a joy to see my parents so relieved, she had started to put on weight, and the colour had returned to her cheeks. Her nurse had long since departed. All she now wanted to do, quite understandably, was to join up in one of the women's services, but she was not quite fit enough to do that yet and this made her very dejected poor girl. Her doctors wanted to be absolutely certain before she took this step and so it meant having to wait and be patient.

I would like to tell you about her mysterious recovery, for her cure was carried out without a single blessing from any of her specialists and doctors, in fact they warned my father that if anything went wrong, then he must expect to take the full blame. She was cured by Abraham's Magic Black Box! Apparently this man was regarded as somewhat of a crank, way back in the First World War when he invented his black box treatment. At that time my mother had a very nasty ulcerated tongue which failed to respond to any medical treatment. So my father took her to this man's Harley Street Clinic – where after three weeks of his treatment her problem had totally disappeared, so obviously my parents had great faith in this black box.

After years of watching their daughter Audrey become weaker and weaker with a form of ulcerative colitis, which no doctor seemed to have produced a cure for, my father announced that if he could find anyone with one of Abraham's black boxes he was at least going to give it a try. They were appalled that he would be so foolish as to dabble, as they put it, with this form of hokum pokum, with someone so ill as his daughter. But nothing would deter him, and he advertised in *The Times* newspaper for someone who might still have one of these magic boxes hidden away beneath the cobwebs in their attics. Within two days he had been offered three – the nearest one being in Brighton, Sussex, so he drove down there and collected it. He couldn't wait to set it up in Audrey's room and so be able to start her off on her course of treatment. We were all so curious to set eyes on this magic box and we hovered around Audrey's bed in anticipation. It was a very ordinary black wooden box with a red electric light bulb attached to the lid. Inside was a hodge podge of electrical wiring resembling a telephone exchange – there were two electrodes, and the idea was to place these in strategic positions on Audrey, one I recall was placed on her tummy. My father then switched it on, and Audrey was well and truly wired up for the unknown. The red light bulb went on and off at a regular rhythm, and we all stood on the spot mesmerised. It had to remain on for a given time, twenty minutes I seem to recall. Dear God, I prayed, do let it work and make her better. I am sure the same fervent prayer was in everyone's heart.

From being an incredibly sick little girl who could no longer walk, over the following months, with this treatment twice a day, she grew into a bonny happy teenager with the world at her feet. There was no logic to the magic box, perhaps it was merely faith in its mystic powers, who knows? But it did the trick. Eventually she joined the YWCA and served behind the counter in the YMCA where as a result she made many friends, for she was a pretty girl with a lovely smile. She finally joined the MTC (Motor Transport Corps) in 1943.

Audrey's weekly task, and believe me it was a task, for I had done it myself on the odd occasion, was to take a trip to Peasmarsh – midway between Guildford and Godalming. It involved a long downhill walk of well over a mile to town to catch the Godalming bus. She would be dropped off out in the middle of nowhere where she had to walk down a country lane to join a straggling queue of people all waiting patiently there for a sole purpose – to buy fresh dog meat.

The procedure was always the same and for anyone with a heart it was a very sad occasion. An old nag or cow would be led out of the field into a shed, there would be a shot and in due course the meat would appear on an old trolley – steaming and by now painted with blobs of green dye to denote that the meat was unfit for human consumption. It would then be butchered and divided up, then everyone would eventually depart with their quota of meat wrapped up in newspaper – just like fish and chips!

For Audrey this was a weekly occurrence and was vitally important for the feeding of our dogs. We used to cut the meat up into cubes and boil it with lots of water in the designated galvanised bucket on the gas ring in the kitchen. A small portion of meat and excellent gravy would be served with baked bread crusts – our dogs loved it and indeed looked incredibly fit on it. The hardest part of this weekly exercise was that she went carrying empty shopping bags and then had to make the return trip lugging heavy bags all the way.

On one such journey, a neighbour of ours, the mother of a former Speaker of the House of Commons, telephoned my mother to ask if Audrey could entertain a GI who had arrived unexpectedly. He came from the United States and was serving in General Patton's third armoured division. His name was Hugh Marcellus Smith Junior. My mother explained that Audrey had to go and collect the dog meat and if the young man was at a loose end then by all means he could go with her.

I can honestly say that I think Hugh had never in his life seen dog meat except perhaps out of a can and he was to become enlightened and no doubt repulsed that afternoon accompanying Audrey to Peasmarsh. His admiration knew no bounds for this pretty young girl he escorted on a trip that involved four buses and a two-hour-long wait in a queue miles from anywhere, just to get dog meat! It all so impressed him that at the end of his short leave he had fallen hook, line and sinker for this pretty and very young English girl.

He came to our house during those few days leave on any pretext he could muster up – finally asking to have a private talk with our father, who just happened to be home himself on a spot of leave. Very naughtily my mother, along with as many of us who could find the space to press our ears against the closed door, heard Hugh say to my father, 'Gee Sir, Audrey's a great little shopper, I've fallen head over heels in love with her and I would like your permission to ask her to marry me.' We couldn't wait to hear father's reply, being a solicitor he pondered over things with great caution and deliberation. How would he get out of this one? We thought he was bound to say no. Mother nudged me and winked, we all waited with baited breath – Audrey was only seventeen and because of her illness had precious little knowledge of life in the big outside world – a world at war at that. Also, wild stories were circulating that American and Canadian service men were marrying British girls after spinning them yarns about their lifestyles back home. If the truth be told they often came from the back woods and Indian reserves, were married, were this, were that – the stories abounded and they didn't make good hearing.

My father, we thought, handled the situation perfectly, by saying that this request was somewhat premature so far as his daughter was concerned, that he felt that it really wouldn't be fair to him. 'You see Hugh,' he continued, 'she has been a very sick girl for several years, she, unlike you, has never had a carefree teenage life because of her illness, she hasn't had a chance to meet with other people of her age, her life is only now just beginning to take off. I appreciate that you are several years older than Audrey and know what you want from life. I suggest that you both wait a full year to see what transpires – write to each other by all means and have an understanding between yourselves, but I suggest we review the situation next year at about this time.' He cleverly managed to sidetrack the issue and I felt that when he told Hugh that it would not be fair on him, that instead of Hugh he really meant himself. But our father had spoken, given what he thought to be wise counselling and Audrey, who I suspected was none too pleased, had to abide by this decision.

Diana was now of an age to go off to boarding school, the same little preparatory school that Audrey and I had been sent to years previously. The school had been forced to move away from the Kent coast, because the Germans were shelling our shores from France (which one could see on a clear day) causing a great deal of damage. They had moved to Corfe Mullen in Dorset. This of course meant that we were no longer permitted to keep Flo on the farm, as she was officially listed as a Nanny she had now become obsolete – despite the fact that for quite some time she had been acting as a Jack of all trades. The country was in desperate need of more women in the ammunition factories, hospitals, the forces and canteens. So Flo was called up into the NAAFI and she became a canteen supervisor in Aldershot. We were all desolate to lose her, she was a treasure and we hadn't before known life without her. Diana's loss too was enormous – for now Enid, our land army girl, had to cope on her own.

This wretched war was tearing the heart of our nation apart, everything we had ever known, the set pattern of things, it was all disintegrating, just like a dandelion clock, when blown, is carried away on the wind. We missed Flo dreadfully as you can imagine, for she was a strong woman who thrived on hard work and who could turn her hand to anything. The bigger the challenge, the better she liked it. Another string to her bow being that she was a superb needlewoman. Flo's departure obviously meant added strains for my mother – but she never lost her indomitable spirit.

Our second harvest was carried out with the help of eight Canadian soldiers, all agricultural workers from the middle west, and we did it in less than half the time taken the previous year, but with every bit as much fun. In those days the corn had to be stooked and what a pretty sight this made, golden pyramids on a cloth of paler gold, brilliant in the daytime, fading to an even paler shade with orange glints as the sunset sky slowly slipped behind the horizon. To wander through these stooks with someone very special is a memory I shall never wish to forget.

Talking of stooks, my father had managed to organise some leave to help with the harvest, for he enjoyed it as much as we did. A group of us would move up the cut corn field and arrange the stooks in clumps; it had been a good day's work and we had all trundled back to the farmhouse to partake of Nellie's delicious supper. Halfway through the meal my father announced that he had lost his signet ring. It was a treasured possession for he had been given it by his parents on his twenty-first birthday and it had been through thick and thin with him in the trench warfare of the First World War. He said 'I am certain that I had it on my finger before I started to stook the corn, yes – that's where I've lost it, somewhere amongst those stooks.' 'Well, you can't search through every stook Irving,' said my mother. 'Well, I'm certainly going to have a jolly good try,' replied my father. And he did – we all did. I swear there was no stook that wasn't shaken and turned upside down, but to no avail and I knew just how sad he was feeling at losing it, he really was loath to be parted from it. I would see him years after walking that particular field and I knew that he just hoped that some miracle would take place and he would see it shining on the soil.

It was just after harvest time, the autumn had appeared wearing her golden gown and Warren Farm House and her occupants lay peacefully sleeping in the early dawn light. Not my mother though, for she was our night watchman. She had brewed herself a cup of tea and was looking out of the window, taking in the sheer beauty of the early morn when to her great surprise she thought she saw a movement along the ditch in one of our fields alongside the house. No, it couldn't be she thought – but, yes, there was she became alert and watchful, moving cautiously to the next window to get a clearer view. Were they German parachutists she wondered as she stared, transfixed. Yes, there was definitely something going on. She could now clearly spot a clump of moving heather above the top of the ditch – in fact several clumps of heather. Instead of hiding herself away as you might expect, she threw her dressing gown on and went outside carrying a large stick, climbing over a five bar gate to investigate. There, making their way along the bottom of the deep ditch on their bellies, were soldiers, one following the other. My mother, uncertain of who they were exactly, called out 'What on earth are you doing in the bottom of my ditch?' With which one young officer jumped up full of confusion and apologies, for they had obviously not seen her coming – good thing she wasn't a German! He tried to explain to her that they were part of a vast mock war operation, it was of the greatest importance and they could all be courts-martialled if they were seen talking to civilians. 'To hell with that,' said my mother, 'stop your fun and games – you all look as though you could do with a good bath and brush up, followed by a good old fashioned English breakfast.' Although protesting, mildly and ignored I may say by my mother, they meekly followed her into the house. There were twenty of them, Canadians of course, who by good fortune had found a real live Canadian lady miles from anywhere, who was willing to befriend them – to hell with a courts-martial!

I happened to be at home on leave, so before we knew it a party was in the making. Firstly they all took baths, followed by a slap up breakfast. When my father came home his first job was to unblock the bath waste pipe – it had been blocked with heather though how or why he could never understand and my mother never enlightened him.

That evening around eleven o'clock when they departed to reform with the rest of their regiment – behind schedule – my mother looked them fair and square in the eyes and said, 'Now boys, I am banking on you to make sure that none of my chickens or ducks disappear.' Strangely enough we were the only family in a large radius who did not loose a single feathered friend, when all around us people were reporting heavy losses.

Flo telephoned us one day to say that she was going to get married to a Warrant Officer in the Army. By this time she was in her mid-thirties, and my parents were concerned over this momentous step that she was undertaking. My father was to give her away and the reception was to be held at Warren Farm House. Naturally, Nellie was to be her bridesmaid, along with Diana. Endless discussions followed on how we were going to dress Nellie for this important occasion. The final decision was that I would lend her a pre-war dance frock. It was a very delicate apricot silk taffeta with coffee lace puffed sleeves and silk frills, lace formed the front of the dress almost like a long apron. There was only one problem, Nellie could not see eye to eye with the bodice of the frock. There was a good two-inch gap along the side opening, which no way could we fill in, so on the great day there was nothing for it but to stitch her up in it with button thread. This we did with tremendous difficulty, she found it difficult to breathe and totally impossible to laugh. To see her in this feminine straight jacket reduced us to uncontrollable laughter. 'Oh, do stop it everyone' cried Nellie, 'I am in agonies and the thought of having to spend hours in this dress is driving me mad – what if the thread should break, have any of you thought of that?' 'Of course it won't break Nellie,' I said. 'Why, I've used two thicknesses of thread, just hold yourself in and you'll be all right.' She looked so pretty and Flo looked radiant, it was indeed a very happy day.

Sadly the marriage failed. When Flo was expecting her baby her husband left her for another woman. This was indeed a desolate period for Flo and after her daughter Diana was born, my father went and fetched them both from Torquay and brought them back home to the farm and the family – her family. Poor Flo, if nothing else she got what she wanted most of all from life, a real live baby of her very own – but she hadn't bargained for her unfaithful husband.

By this time I had actually met George Pushman for the first time, we had dinner together, our friendship flourished apace and matrimony was our destiny. On top of her many pressures my mother was determined to make certain that her first born had the best send off possible. She entered enthusiastically into the wedding preparations, the purchasing of my wedding dress and trousseau. I, by this time, was stationed in Oxfordshire at RAF Brize Norton and all our plans had to be made by telephone. I had to try and wangle days off to fit in with her non-pigswill collecting days!

We would arrange to meet in London at Harrods, where we behaved like a couple of lovesick girls browsing through all the gossamer silk nighties and lingerie. Somehow even in 1943 Harrods had managed to obtain some heavenly things and my mother got completely carried away. Perhaps it was because her own wedding in October 1916 had been such a hurried affair, with my father dashing home from the Front to snatch a couple of days before returning to the grim battlefields of France. But whatever the reason she was making certain that only the very best was good enough for her daughter.

We didn't find a wedding dress on that particular occasion, so off we set again on our search the following week. As we approached the Bridal Department at Bourne and Hollingsworth there it was in all its Victorian glory dressed out on a stand for all to admire – especially we two dreamy girls! It was just what I had always dreamed of having, stiff spotted muslin, with a very full tiered skirt – leg o' mutton sleeves and a tight-fitting bodice. The veil was silk French net edged with a double frill of narrow spotted lace and the headpiece was a posy of forget-me-nots and orange blossom. We looked at each other and smiled from ear to ear. 'Oh mother, it's gorgeous,' I said with a deep sigh, 'now all we have to worry about is will it fit me?' Of course it fitted, just perfectly, as though it had been made for me and as I appeared in it, everyone standing around with curiosity (for everyone goes goofy over a bride) started to clap with oh's and ah's of approval.

We had a very successful day at Bournes, where I managed to select the greater part of my trousseau. In those days hats, gloves and bags to match each outfit had to be chosen. To find attractive shoes in wartime was a nightmare, especially if you had long narrow feet such as I had. In fact it made one spit chips to see a London prostitute mincing along in a divine pair of patent shoes, for one knew full well one of her American servicemen customers had got them for her from the USA. One thing I did have was a pair of heavenly pure silk French cami knickers from Harrods, which I was to wear to go away in. They were pale pink silk with ecru fine lace and pale blue satin lover's knots – they cost the earth, but were worth every penny. I have now made them into a scatter cushion for my bed!

Mother always chuckled when my father used to query some account that would come in years after our wedding and would just say to him, 'Oh it's part of Muriel's wedding darling!' He always seemed to accept it.

My two sisters were to be my bridesmaids, and they were to wear apricot silk taffeta bridesmaids dresses that Audrey and I had worn to a swish society London wedding just before the war. They had only been worn on the one occasion and they were very pretty.

The excitement was beginning to mount as the replies to the invitations were starting to pour in. I had asked some of my favourite WAAFs if they would like to form a guard of honour. It was nice to have them with me on that special day. The Officer's Mess had collected money, which they presented to me to choose a present. We chose a lovely long silver cigarette box, which we had inscribed. Being wartime meant that we received mostly cheques as wedding gifts, apart from lovely pieces of silver. We only in fact had one duplication, and that was six sets of fish servers, which came in handy for giving as presents at other weddings!

George sadly had no relatives in England, so he invited his Squadron and Air Officer Commanding, Sir Basil Embry. He also had a bevy of very glamorous WAAF officers who came to give him moral support. His best man was to be Major Colin Gray. I had a terrific send off from Brize Norton on the start of my leave, and I gather that George did too, from all accounts his party continued until a few hours before the wedding — a real bachelor's night out!

We had to make an early start from Guildford on the morning of the wedding. I had a hair appointment in London and with thick hair it took hours to dry. My mother was to collect my wedding dress and it had been arranged that everyone should meet up at The Butcher's Livery Hall at noon for a cold lunch. The plan was for Flo, Nellie, Audrey and Diana to catch a later train. I was too excited to eat any lunch, I think we all were.

We started to put our glad rags on, my time was fully occupied making up Flo and Nellie and fixing their hats, when I realised that the time was ticking on and I hadn't even started to get myself dressed.

My sister Diana had worked herself up into a tizzy, usually a sign
of nervous tension, and she began to sulk saying that she didn't want
to be a bridesmaid after all – she was nine and could be the very
devil. Heading out to the car with my mother and Audrey she flung
her bouquet down on the pavement and stamped her foot refusing
to get into the car. 'Right Diana,' said my mother, 'we are going to
leave you here, Muriel wouldn't want a sulking bridesmaid.' With
which she got into the car good as gold.

I often wonder if brides can honestly say that they can remember in detail the walk up the aisle – the thoughts going through
their minds, the service and the signing of the register. For me it was
mostly a cloudy hazy dream, but I remember walking down the aisle
to the wedding march with complete clarity, my nervousness had
disappeared, I hadn't fluffed my responses and wonder of all wonders
I was now Mrs George Rupert Pushman. This indeed was a wonderful day.

The service had its amusing moments. In the vestry whilst signing the register, our best man, Major Colin Gray of the Queens
Regiment, was trying to organise his bridesmaids into some form
of order, no doubt on military lines. However, he had not bargained
for the headstrong young bridesmaid which he very soon found out
he had on his hands. He suggested to her that she should walk down
the aisle behind me so as to see to my train – and that he and Audrey
would follow. She swung round glaring up at him defiantly saying,
'I certainly won't!' Colin was flabbergasted and replied, 'And why
not Diana?' 'Well, how do I know you won't kick me?' was her reply.
This was all too much for the Major, never before had such a suggestion been made to this elegant soldier. She did in fact follow me
down the aisle but our walk was hazardous to say the very least, for
each time she turned round to glare at him, she stepped on my train
causing our little procession to grind to a halt and it was a miracle
that my veil stayed put!

We came out into sunshine on this glorious August day, and there
were my WAAF friends lined up smartly on each side of the pathway.

There were groups of curious onlookers, the sort one always sees at weddings, photographers, the odd stray mongrel dog, even a sailor and we all know it brings good luck should one touch his collar – so I did! Finally to set the scene a dear old London policeman. All wished us well, on this our own special day, Saturday 14 August 1943 at St Bartholomew The Great Church, London. It was lovely to see friends at the reception that we had not seen for years, and to think that they had made the effort to travel, despite the difficulties of the bombings, lengthy delays and diversions, to be with us on that day. We finally said our farewells, leaving the obvious makings of a happy party, to spend the night at The Dorchester Hotel on Park Lane, and on the following day, continue our journey to Cornwall.

During our honeymoon George was recalled from leave. His squadron were facing critical times, in fact his friends had been unable to attend our wedding due to a special low-level raid they had had to undertake. It had resulted in disaster for many, for flying in at low level to avoid detection on the radar, they had unwittingly flown into a swarm of locusts which when hitting their windscreens had blotted out their vision. They were forced to increase their height and in doing that they were then targets for the German ack ack guns.

One of George's friends, who luckily managed to escape capture, was passed down the French Resistance Line, having to trudge over the Pyrenees non-stop to reach the safety of Spain and the British Embassy in Madrid. Once there he was glancing idly through a copy of *The Tatler* magazine and who should he see but his old friend George Pushman and his new bride Muriel on their wedding day coming out of St Bartholomew The Great Church. To think he, too, should have been there. Bill was one of the lucky ones and arrived back in the mess one month to the day later.

9

GROWING FAMILY

Three months after my marriage I had to bid farewell to the
WAAF for I became pregnant. I had mixed feelings about leaving, for I had spent a wonderful three years in the Service and I
realised that going home would not be easy, for it meant leaving
all my friends behind. Knowing at the same time that my pre–war
friends in and around Guildford would be away, some were married,
whilst others were, like me, in the Armed Forces. I would have to
give up this way of life that I had really come to love, for life on the
farm. Would it have lost some of its glamour for me, I wondered?

Also, the prospect of becoming a mother was somewhat awesome,
for I felt that as yet I was an immature wife! Meetings since our wedding had been few and far between. George's squadron was working
flat out, it was, after all, a hectic time in the skies. To crown it all I felt
terribly sick and queasy all the time. On those rare occasions that we
did meet up George was, quite naturally, ready for a party, when all I
wanted to do was hang my head over a bucket! Luckily my period of
malaise only lasted until I was five months into my pregnancy; after
that I perked up and was ready to tackle anything.

I can recall my father calling me into the morning room, a thing
he always did when he had something of importance to say, to give
me a 'Britain needs you'-type pep talk. 'My dear,' he started, 'now
that you are over your morning sickness, I don't want to see you sitting about around the house with no particular purpose in life, why
don't you go down to the recruiting office and see if you can get a

job as a factory supervisor? You have the right qualifications for that and it will help to keep your mind off worrying about George and his flying.' Well, I took a deep gulp and considered his suggestion with suppressed laughter. Here I was beginning to look like a fertile turtle and in those far away days there was precious little to choose from in the way of maternity clothes. Women seemed to become very private during their bulging period and the best offer in the shops were maternity smocks, which were usually brightly flowered, voluminous half overalls which made one look like a whale – and, by the by, they always had long sleeves! Wanting to appear different I wore my pretty pyjama tops and a skirt of pre-war antiquity which I sewed tapes onto – as I grew in girth so I released the tapes. 'Father,' I said, choosing my words carefully, 'I haven't felt like doing anything since I left the WAAF and now that I am feeling so much better I have a thousand and one things to do to prepare for the arrival of our baby. There is a lot of shopping to do for one thing and I want to start sewing the layette, you know me, I can't wait to get started. In any case I want to be home when George gets leave, I am sure you can appreciate that.' Well, that seemed to satisfy him, and the subject was soon forgotten.

Audrey by this time had joined the MTC – The Motor Transport Corps – and was at long last in uniform. She turned many heads I can tell you. I was so happy for her, because it was the fervent wish of most girls of the time to get into uniform and she had really had to bide her time through no fault of her own.

Diana was away at school and causing havoc we were led to understand, she was an irrepressible tomboy, who could gather like-minded girls around her as though she were the Pied Piper of Hamlin.

My dearest grandmother had died suddenly the previous February from influenza, which had cast a sad shadow over everyone at Warren Farm House, for despite her age she had made her presence felt in a gentle and dignified manner. She had missed my wedding and now, at a time when I would have loved to have joined her by her fireside, her wing of the house lay cold and empty.

Unbeknown to me my parents had discussed offering us granny's flat to live in, so that we could have our own little unit. It came therefore as a wonderful surprise when they told us of their plan, for it held so many happy memories for me and I knew that I would never feel lonely there when George was away flying for she had left her imprint in every room.

How very different my life was now compared to those fast moving fun days in uniform. I had indeed been right when I expressed my doubts about returning to life as a civilian – and pregnant to boot! Of course I wanted to have a baby, but at the same time I was young and wanted to be in the middle of things – to have a good time. Was it asking for too much I asked myself?

George was, of course, away flying his aeroplanes, and I knew only too well what good times he would be having back at the mess – after all – had I not known what mess life was all about? But, as my mother would have said, 'Muriel, stop moaning and feeling sorry for yourself, you're pregnant, now pull yourself together and make the most of it!' I took myself down to Guildford and had a wonderful spending spree. I was able to buy lovely pre-war baby clothes from Whites the drapers, I had always dreamed of dressing my baby in long clothes and here they were just waiting for me to come and buy them. The fad for up to date baby clothes had just about begun, so there was no demand for long dresses and petticoats that would take a lot of ironing. They were made by a firm called Happy Days and they were beautiful – I even found some long flannelette petticoats; it never occurred to me that my baby, due in June, would be quite warm enough without flannelette!

George used to come home whenever he could get off – even if only for a few hours. Luckily he was stationed only twenty miles away at Hartford Bridge near Camberley and the joy of his unexpected arrivals turned the whole house upside down. My father used to call the house 'Kissing Castle' whenever George came home. Nellie would be in a whirl, fussing around him and spoiling him outrageously. Apart from loving him very much, it was a total relief to know that he was still alive – quite something I can assure you in those dreadful times.

He was on low-level raids, his plane just skimming the channel seas to avoid being picked up by radar. They would hug the green fields and hedge hop, suddenly having to zoom up to fly over cables and buildings, this meant that they had to be constantly on the alert, and extreme concentration was demanded under these tense conditions.

Puffing Billy was ceremoniously handed over to George by my father to enable him to nip home at a moment's notice and the two of them became inseparable. George used to reckon on average seventeen miles to the puncture! For annoyances such as this he seemed to have unending patience and over the months to follow became a dab hand at mending the punctures. It involved keeping a large bottle of water in the car, a bucket and a repair kit. First off would come the wheel, the tyre removed and the inner tube tested in a bucket of water to find the hole. It would then be dried gently like a baby's bottom and the repair kit instructions carried out to the n'th degree; the inner tube tucked once more into the tyre and finally the wheel replaced. It wasn't the sort of job for a chap when he was dressed up to the nines taking his wife out to a party, but he always managed to laugh it off – that was George.

On many occasions Puffing Billy would be crammed full of George's squadron friends, all coming to partake of one of my mother's famous Warren Farm House dinners. These were carefree days when George was away from his aeroplane, we could all relax for a few hours at least.

The war had become more intense and it was obvious that things were building up to a crescendo. My baby was officially due on 6 June. There was one party at the mess which I so wanted to attend – it was to celebrate George being promoted to Squadron Leader. However, I looked such a funny shape and my maternity clothes left a lot to be desired and above all I didn't want to let George down. How could I look my best for George? I rummaged through my meagre wardrobe, but it has to be remembered that the war had been going on for four years and during the majority of this time I had only worn uniform and my pre-war clothes had been purchased then to fit a willowy slim girl. I came across a very pretty black dress that I had always liked to wear on special occasions, but with all the will in the world the side zip just would not close. I asked Nellie to come and give me her honest opinion, but I didn't really want to hear it for I knew exactly what she was going to say – so I got in first. 'Nellie,' I said, 'you have some corsets haven't you, can I borrow them please?' 'Oh! I don't know what to say Muriel, do you think you should try and squeeze yourself into them, I don't think your mother would let you, you know. It's not that you can't borrow them, of course you can, but I am just worried that they will be too tight.' She fetched them though and between us we pushed and shoved, with Nellie pulling the laces, and eventually we managed to close the zip. Although I felt as snug as a bug in a rug, I almost felt like my old self again. I said a quick word to our Lord asking him to forgive my vanity and to try to understand just how important it was for me to put my best foot forward that night for George's sake!

I went to the party and had a wonderful time dancing, though secretly I wondered if my baby might arrive that night on the way home. I certainly hoped not, for then my guilt would have known no bounds. What a relief when I reached home and could get out of Nellie's ghastly corsets – they were by now killing me. Our baby daughter in fact arrived on 3 June 1944. This was a piece of good fortune (must have been those tight corsets) for us both. George had been given twenty-four hours leave starting on 2 June, so he was actually at home and was able to drive me to the nursing home, the Mount Alvernia. This place was run by nuns, with efficiency and kindness ruling supreme.

Margaret Anne was born at twenty minutes past ten that evening – and at that time I swore never to have another one! George came to see us once I had been prettied up, for husbands in those days certainly were never allowed within spitting distance of this very female and private business.

Not only did George come to see us – but he also came to say goodbye, for he had received a message to say that all the squadron had to report back to base immediately. It was a sad parting and would have been even more so had we known what a holocaust was about to take place in the early morning of 6 June 1944.

I was in a four-bedded room called St Rose, everything was a pretty shade of pale pink – the sheets, satin eiderdown, the walls, the china and our babies' pink flounced cots which were hooked onto the sides of our beds. We were kept in bed for two weeks, just being allowed to get up to bath and change our babies during the last few days.

In the morning we were all sitting up in bed when suddenly we became aware of a sinister noise in the sky close by. Whatever it was, it was certainly evil and a note of fear flowed from one mother to another in that pretty pink room. The door suddenly burst open and a nursing nun, Sister Concepta, called to us to get out of our beds and take our babies in our arms and get underneath the beds as quickly as we could. We did it without hesitation, though the sinister noise had ceased as suddenly as it had come. There was an enormous bang followed by blast shock waves. 'Oh! God,' we all exclaimed in unison as we huddled there. 'What on earth has happened?' for the explosion seemed to be very close. We must have made an amusing sight had the occasion not been so frightening, for there we were, all shapes and sizes, crouched under our beds clasping brand new babies that we had very little experience in handling. Margaret was only twelve hours old – what an entrance into this crazy and sinister world I thought.

Our attire was also very cumbersome, for we were bound up tightly with linen binders, rather like roller towels, which were supposed to push our tummies back into shape. We wore colossal sanitary towels for the first week which felt far from secure as we huddled there – no, this was not a happy moment in our new roles as mothers. I only hoped that someone would come in and tell us what had happened – the suspense was awful.

Rumours, as they always do, started flying about – and rumour said this was a new and sinister device called a flying bomb, known later as 'buzz bombs'. They were unmanned small aeroplanes loaded with high explosives, they would fly on their evil mission on a con-trolled flight path, the engine would cut out and the entire thing would drop like a stone creating the most awful carnage below.

One got to know their familiar engine sound, whereupon eve-ryone had to dive for shelter just in case it decided to cut out. One never could be certain when it would cut out, there was no warning of any sort. Unfortunately, the Guildford area happened to be on one of their flight paths to Greater London. The one thing that the war years taught us was caution.

As I lay in my bed at the nursing home on the morning of 6 June, we were to hear on the radio that the Allied Forces were landing on the beaches in Normandy. There we were, four young mothers, each with a husband somewhere on the battle front. We felt like crying, but what good would that do? Praying for their safety would be more to the point. The overall feeling was one of great jubilation that our men were out there fighting for us all, but deep, deep down we all feared the price that was having to be paid for our freedom. One thing was certain, at this time in our history any battle was battle to the death.

I would look down at my innocent baby as pretty as a little rosebud and wonder whether she would ever see her father. Self pity would then creep in – after all, one tends to become weepy after having had a baby whatever the circumstances and we had all these extra worries to con-tend with. What if I should be widowed as all too many girls of my age were? The thought of the loneliness terrified me and yet, when I pon-dered deeply about the situation, I felt I really hardly knew my husband, his family or his past history. Our courtship, just like everyone else's in wartime, was brief to say the very least – just one big fling in an unreal world. We had spent so little time together and when we did it was to dash off to some party or another and the time for serious talking never arose. I wondered, if I should be widowed, who would want to marry me with a tiny baby. I turned on my side away from the other mothers and cried bitterly into my pillow for all I knew at that moment was that I loved him above all else and I wanted him so desperately to be spared to come home to the farm, to Margaret and to me.

On D-Day plus two, the worst was to happen in our pretty lit-tle room. Through the door came a colonel and an army chaplain escorted by Sister Concepta – heading towards the bed of one of the mothers, who had just given birth to her third baby. It was to tell her that her husband had been killed on the landing beach named Arromanches on D-Day. She was grief-stricken. Indeed we all were, for how could we be happy, when the life of one of us could never be the same again? I got out of bed along with the other mothers and we took her shaking body into our arms, trying to ease the appalling pain she was going through. Each of us thinking deep down that perhaps we too had become widows. The grim scenario was just too awful to contemplate. Day by day passed with no news from our loved ones until the restrictions of silence were lifted fourteen days later.

My father fetched us home. We had had no news from George, their bases were sealed to the outside world and in any case he was flying almost non-stop. His squadron had been responsible for laying a smoke screen over the battleships bombing the French coast near Le Havre. Imagine then my ecstatic joy and relief when George turned up on the doorstep – on my birthday, 13 June – my lucky number and indeed my very lucky day. It was only a fleeting visit, but we were all together again and fear was forgotten for twenty-four hours.

I recall an incident that night. My father was talking to George about the flying bombs, which as yet George had not experienced. It was late at night and we were sitting around a huge log fire with the men sipping their whiskies. We stopped talking to listen, suddenly alert as foxes – yes, it was what we thought. 'There is one coming now,' said my father, 'Hurry up and fetch little Margaret, we must all dash for the shelter, I'll fetch Aunt Lilah – we must all run for our lives.' George stood up saying, 'What's all the panic for Pop? It's only a Lancaster bomber going over.' 'Bomber be damned,' responded my father, as we all piled into the shelter. With that the engine on this monster cut out, there was a sound of gushing wind as it passed over the house followed by the familiar bang! I can assure you that George hopped into our shelter with no more objections! The bomb landed in a quiet residential road, killing a harmless old couple in their beds – all for the purpose of wearing down our morale.

That summer turned into a nightmare. I would just have my baby in her bath, all slippery with soap when one of these wretched things would fly over or the air-raid siren would sound. I would have to gather her up as best I could in a towel and dash for our lives at top speed to reach the shelter in time. It always seemed to happen at the worst possible time – I breast-fed her, so that always raised difficulties – so much so that I decided to feed her in our shelter – hoping that no one would come in, as I differed from Mrs Bill in this respect. The other worry was putting her to bed, then having to grab her and rush for the safety of the shelter just as she had dropped off to sleep. Strangely, despite all these unnatural disturbances she grew up to be an incredibly placid and unflappable girl.

The most nerve-wracking aspect of these times, which affected the entire family, was the fact that George's squadrons used to fly directly over the house and gardens when setting off on a raid – sometimes flying several sorties a day. My mother and I, Flo and Nellie would dash out into the garden when we heard the familiar engine sounds and wave up to them in a pretty futile manner, for they obviously couldn't see us. Somehow I knew that George would be thinking of us before turning his concentration fully onto the job in hand. This gave me some form of comfort during this extremely tense time. The nerve-wracking bit was trying to busy oneself until we heard their planes returning – we would all dash out again and count the number of aircraft. More often than not we would find one, two, three or maybe more missing. Mother sensing my thoughts would give me a cheerful smile and try and reassure me that George was sure to be amongst the survivors. 'Darling, George is a born survivor,' she would say putting her arm around me. I would wait nervously and impatiently for the telephone to ring, sometimes hours later.

We lived this hell on earth all summer and autumn long and I think it began to take its toll, for this was merely existing, not really living, as one day melted into another. Often in fact the planes had become separated during the raid and as a result came home under their own steam – at least, that is what George told me and though it was a nice thought it certainly wasn't always the case. As a result of that nightmare time I developed a hatred of aircraft and I promised myself all those years ago never to fly if I could avoid it.

On a lighter note – one day my father was digging in the garden when a plane came over giving the odd dip with its wings. He naturally assumed that it was old George, as he used to call him, when suddenly a large piece of goodness knows what came away from beneath the aeroplane. He and Diana dived into the ditch for shelter imagining it to be some sort of bomb. However, there was no explosion, so very slowly they surfaced and advanced to investigate – upon inspection they found it to be a panel from the floor of the aeroplane. It turned out to be George's – and they were able to hand it back to him!

George would sometimes telephone me to say that we were going to some mess party, telling me to be ready and waiting in my glad rags for him to pick me up in Puffing Billy. I would feed Margaret and leave her in my mother's tender care and go to the party. As the night progressed I would find my 'dairy' becoming intensely uncomfortable, so would slip away heading for home to relieve this situation. George would hold my dress up high above my head to save having to remove it, I would then feed Margaret and burp her, rearrange my dress, and hand her once more into my mother's care. We would return to the party at Puffing Billy's special top speed – hopefully with no punctures along the way!

It was certainly a fast moving, crazy era. Life seemed to be lived to the full every single day, for there just might not be a tomorrow. We girls at home were either riding on a high or being flung down into the deepest troughs of despair. The calm middle course was unknown to us. When would this awful war end we all wondered?

At the time when Margaret was christened, George had been, reluctantly, taken off operations for a period of rest. He invited the new crew of his beloved Boston aircraft to come to the Christening party. It was such a happy day, spent entirely in the garden at Warren Farm House. One boy that I particularly remember was a Canadian by the name of Pete Vickers. He seemed to just stand spellbound beside Margaret's pram all afternoon, saying in wonderment, 'Isn't she so beautiful, just look at her little fingers.' Just the following day the entire crew went missing, believed killed over Normandy, and that was the tragic ending of that. There was no answer, you either lived or you died.

After this sad experience, which was really too close for comfort, I was not only relieved but extremely grateful that George had been taken off operations, even if he wasn't. One could breathe again freely. However, this happiness was not to last for long, for George was posted to Brussels in Belgium, and once again I had to face the fear of losing him and suffer months of separation.

I, of course, was not the only one – some women had been parted from their husbands for years and a fear for many of them was that even if he did make it back they would have grown up and apart. Sadly this did frequently happen, through nobody's fault. A lot of men swore never to marry in wartime and I must admit that I had had misgivings about it myself. In a way I was lucky for at least I had my family all around me, but human nature is such that you always want the one person you cannot have!

My mother's health was beginning to deteriorate and I was desperately sad to see this brilliant star slowly losing its light. The willpower was there, but quite simply the strength was not. A small stroke or two caused her to step one rung back down the ladder of life. My father was still away in MI5, now at Blenheim Palace, Woodstock near Oxford. He made a point of coming home whenever he could, but somehow he just never seemed to be there when he really was most needed.

Audrey was writing daily to her American boyfriend, whose division was pushing forward towards the Rhine. She missed him dreadfully and as I knew exactly how she felt my heart went out to her. The only good bit of news at this point was that Flo was back at the farm, to relieve my poor weary mother.

Christmas that year was spent as all our Christmas's had been spent, but somehow some of the sparkle was missing. My father had driven around Guildford gathering up lonely soldiers who were aimlessly wandering around the town for want of something better to do. Maybe it was because we were all older, or perhaps it was because we were all

utterly sick to death of the war, but it was as though we were play acting that year. So many of our friends and neighbours and their children
had been killed, or taken prisoner of war, or just simply 'missing'.

My mother's health was failing, and it was very hard for us to come
to terms with it. We had thought her immortal – she just had to be
to hold us all together. George was in Brussels, Audrey was pining for
her sweetheart, Flo was married to a man who'd left her for another
woman. No, things were certainly not the same and try as we would
we could never recapture the enchantment of those early war years.

With the Christmas decorations packed lovingly away for another
year, life carried on at the farm as usual. George was managing to get
home, albeit briefly, once a month. Audrey was driver to the secretary to the Minister of Supply and so was away all day, and of course
Diana was at boarding school. Our evacuees had long since departed
leaving just my mother, myself and Margaret, Aunt Lilah, Flo and her
baby Diana, Nellie and finally Enid our Land Army girl. The only
male amongst us was Bill, our cowman, who had been released from
his wartime duties with the War Agricultural Committee.

Our canine population seemed to be the only one on the increase.
When George asked me to marry him I have a strange suspicion that
he was not only after a wife, but a wife with a mother who would take
on his pregnant bitch as part of his dowry! She was a dear called Havoc,
who used to fly with him when he was buzzing about Britain in his
light communication aircraft called a Havoc – 'Cry Havoc and let loose
the dogs of war'. In due course she produced a huge litter of collie puppies. Audrey kept one which she called Flack and I chose the cutest little
black bitch with a white powder puff tip to her tail, four white paws, a
crisp white shirt front and one ear that flopped over – I called her Judy.

I must pay tribute to my dear father who had to put up with a
granddaughter who picked the flower heads off his prize tulips and
puppies who attempted to dig through his precious lawn to Australia!

The only comforting news at the time was that we appeared to be
winning the war, so with a great deal of optimism and plenty of faith
in the good Lord, we hoped it would all be over very soon.

10

VICTORY IN EUROPE

Finally it was over – we were victorious in Europe. What a wild and jubilant night VE celebrations turned out to be. George was at home and we gathered up Audrey and Flo and the four of us headed for Guildford High Street at top speed – where it appeared that we were joined by the entire town. We were all going wild with joy, excitement and sheer relief. We danced in the streets, even bringing our drinks out of the pubs and raising our glasses to complete strangers who had suddenly become our life-long buddies. We sang and we cried for those who would not be coming home and for the release of all our pent-up emotions. Policemen had their helmets tossed around like rugby balls, but they cared not, for this was a precious moment to be savoured to the full.

George, who always had crazy ideas, suggested that we drive up to the White Hart at Nettlebed, near Henley on Thames – a good hour's journey by car. He had been stationed at Wallingford a year previously and there was not a man in Air Force blue who did not love 'Clemmie', the wonderful lady who ran the White Hart. She had been every officer's friend and confidante, and we knew that everyone who could make it would be at Clemmie's that night – and we were right! It was a monumental party, and she was in her element with all her boys around her. I felt as though it was almost a farewell party, for, from now on, people would be demobilised and would return to their pre-war occupations, probably never to meet up again.

Above: The marriage of Irving and Florence, Muriel's mother and father, London 1916, with Irving's parents and their best man, Guy Richardson. Florence was always known as Monty.

Right: Monty Gane (right) with a friend, both in the uniform of the Queen Alexandra Army Nursing Corps. Monty served as a theatre sister during the First World War, having come over from Canada in 1915. In later years, in the event of any member of her family becoming ill she would immediately assume her efficient nursing manner and, putting her skills and knowledge to use, would inspire great confidence in her power to care for them.

Above: Muriel Gane, born on 13 June 1921. She is pictured in her christening robe, a robe that was used by many generations of the family.

Left: Audrey Gane, aged eight, was a bridesmaid at the London wedding of Colin Sneath and Nancie Gilbert in 1934. Audrey is pictured with the best man, Peter Sneath. Her dress was wine red velvet and she had autumn-coloured flowers on her headband and in her bouquet.

Muriel, Audrey and Daddy at the beach at Kingsdown near Deal. This was half-term holiday from St Monica's school. This was their only weekend away that year as weekends and half-terms were spent at the school, as was Easter, if it happened to fall in term-time.

Diana Montgomery Mary Gane was born on 20 January 1934. She was thirteen years younger than her oldest sister Muriel. She had to grow up very quickly when war began and did not have the opportunity to enjoy the lifestyle that her older sisters had taken for granted when they were children.

Audrey and her mother and father haymaking in the summer of 1935. Audrey would have been nine.

4

The family nanny, Flo, with Diana
in one of the fields around Warren
Farm House in 1936.

Pluto, one of the family's many
animals, 'our guardian angel'.

The dining room at Warren Farm House, in 1937. The room was converted for use as Audrey's bedroom during her illness. The floodwater also came rushing in through these French doors and windows.

Opposite: Muriel at seventeen years old in 1938.

Warren Farm House, surrounded by 180 acres of land when Muriel lived there. The upstairs window shown in this photograph was Muriel's bedroom window. The man was Old Thomas, who cut the hay with a scythe.

Warren Farm House. The oldest section (central part) was said to have been an inn in Chaucer's time, alongside the Pilgrim's Way. The left side dates from Tudor times and the right side of the building (not shown here) is Georgian.

Warren Farm House, March 1939 — rear view.

Rear view of Warren Farm House showing the Georgian section of the house — as photographed in 1992.

Above: Lt D. (for Donald) M. Judd, DSC.

Left: Multi-talented Flo is pictured haymaking in 1940.

Below: Muriel undertook her initial training here in Harrogate (the Hotel Majestic) when she joined the WAAF in January 1941.

Muriel, with friend Sgt Pat Miller, May 1942.

Muriel is pictured in the 'quiet garden' outside the family home in the summer of 1942. At this time she was based at Fighter Command HQ, RAF Bentley Priory, Stanmore in Middlesex.

Left: Corporal Muriel
Gane (left) and Warrant
Officer Biddlecombe at
Fighter Command HQ,
Bentley Priory, 1942.

Below: Muriel and her
'best friend' Sally, 1938.

Above: Muriel plays lacrosse at Fighter Command HQ, Stanmore, July 1942.

Below: Muriel won the Women's Inter-services Sports Day Championship in 1941, high-jumping to a height of 5ft 3in.

Six bombs landed around Warren Farm House, on the land and garden, in 1941. The crater in the foreground was caused by a very large bomb.

This crater was left by the explosion of a 500lb bomb in 1941.

A winter wonderland was created in autumn of 1941. This was as a result of a cloud of chalk dust raised by exploding bombs.

'Tiny', Capt. Reg Lang's batman, standing in the bottom of the bomb crater, surrounded by chalk, in 1941.

Above: Florence Gane with two turkeys, which she bred from eggs.

Left: Flo is pictured milking Bluebell in 1942. Flo was much more than a nanny for the family and they all felt her loss greatly when she was called up in 1943.

Opposite above: At Flo's wedding. From left to right: Diana Gane, Nellie (Flo's sister – the family's cook) and Irving Gane. Diana and Nellie were bridesmaids and Irving gave the bride away.

Opposite below: Audrey, outside Warren Farm House.

Back Row (Left to Right): Cadet Brownlee, Cadet Caldwell, Cadet Ellis, Cadet Ferry, Cadet Cadet Bush, Cadet Bowen.

Middle Row (Left to Right): Cadet Hart, Cadet Collis, Cadet James, Cadet Bodie, Cadet Cle Cadet Forster.

Front Row (Left to Right): Cadet Holloway, Cadet Forrester, Cadet Cumming, Cadet Chatte Cadet Alexander, Cadet Bence, Cadet Davenport, Cadet Buchanan.

WAAF O.C.T.U., 19 August 1942 to 16 September 1942. Muriel Gane stands in the back row, seventh from the left.

Cadet R. Hill, Cadet Gane, Cadet Glass, Cadet Worrall, Cadet Hacking, Cadet Young,

et Cave, Cadet Brooks, Cadet Hall, Cadet Binns, Cadet Brent, Cadet Foard, Cadet Garrett,

et Bullough, Cadet Burton, Cadet Crawshaw, Cadet Eaglesfield, Cadet Cobbett, Cadet Brodie

Muriel at Bowness on Windermere, 1943, on a senior WAAF officer's course. Her rank was
SO (section officer).

Above: Penarth School, Wales, May 1943. Muriel was stationed here in Balloon Command as P.T. instructor.

Right: Audrey, aged seventeen, is pictured in the 'quiet garden' at Warren Farm House, in 1943.

The family's nanny, Flo, was called up in 1943. She went into the NAAFI as a charge hand in a canteen at Aldershot.

Flo and Danny on their wedding day,
1943.

Diana Gunn, Flo's only child. She was
named after Diana Gane.

George and Muriel Pushman leave St Bartholomew's The Great Church in the City of London after their wedding on 14 August 1943. The guard of honour were from RAF Brize Norton. Muriel was a section officer stationed there in the WAAF at that time.

Opposite above: Muriel's wedding, with her mother in attendance.

Opposite below: Squadron Leader George Pushman DFC with his Boston crew, 1943, 88 Squadron, Two Group. He stands fourth from the left.

Muriel, on return from honeymoon in 1943.

A happy family moment – George and Muriel with their new baby daughter, who was just three weeks' old, born on 3 June 1944.

26

Above: Margaret's christening, Warren Farm House, 1944. Pictured with George and Muriel are godparents Air Vice-Marshall Sir Basil Embry and Catherine Mayor. Sir Basil was George's Air Officer commanding No.88 Squadron.

Right: Audrey Blanchard Gane, Motor Transport Corps driver, in 1944.

Above: Two family dogs.
Muriel and her sister would
pool their pocket money to
buy puppies at Guildford
cattle market. They were
offspring from George's bitch
Havoc, who would fly with
him on non-operational
flights in the UK.

Left: Audrey and Hugh
Marcellus Smith Junior,
from Binghampton, New
York State, USA, married
in June 1945. They married
at Christ Church, Waterden
Road, Guildford. Hugh was
a GI in General Patton's 3rd
Armoured Division.

Above: Audrey and Hugh's wedding, June 1945.

Below: George, Muriel and Sir Irving Gane are pictured in 1945 after the latter was elected Chamberlain of the City of London.

Above: The *Queen Mary*. This is the ship in which war bride Muriel and daughter Margaret (aged two) travelled from Southampton to Halifax, Nova Scotia, to join George, a journey never to be forgotten.

Left: Nellie, the family's cook, and baby Nigel, who was two weeks old, 1948.

Above: Timothy, Nigel and Margaret Pushman.

Right: Timothy Douglas George Pushman, aged eleven in 1958.

Muriel and George at Arrowmanches D-Day Landing Beach in 1995.

I shall never forget the violent thunderstorm we had to drive through on our way home in the early dawn. It appears that this storm was pretty general, stretching into Europe. I felt it to be almost as though God was issuing a severe warning to us all – that never were we to let destruction on this scale occur again. I was frightened, for it certainly seemed like no ordinary storm.

By June my mother had taken to her bed and really was very unwell. One day we had a most unexpected surprise when Hugh Marcellus Smith Junior arrived on our doorstep – following up a telegram he had sent saying, 'Four days leave, coming to marry Audrey.' 'Come in Hugh,' I said, 'How wonderful to see you and what a surprise! Audrey sadly is at work and will not be home until late and our father is at a dinner in London, in fact Audrey is driving him home.' Imagine their surprise when they arrived home at midnight and Hugh opened the door with a 'Hi Audrey!'

The excitement was immense, but the ensuing problems were complicated to put it mildly! Audrey's nineteenth birthday was only a week away and so she was regarded as a minor in the eyes of the law. In order to get a marriage licence both parents had to sign the necessary forms and here was my mother at this exciting time ill in her bed.

My father wouldn't hear of them only having a two-day honeymoon, so told them that he would arrange everything the next day. He was by nature a great organiser and would never take 'no' for an answer. 'Now you two,' he said, 'I want you to be ready to go to London with me at the crack of dawn and we will take Enid with us as our go between.' What a strange collection of people set off by train for London town – there was my father in his Army Major's uniform, my sister in her khaki uniform tunic, skirt and hat of the MTC, our Land Army girl Enid in her smart breeches, forest green jumper, kneelength socks and regulation hat, and, of course, last but certainly not least the bridegroom to be, Hugh, in his GI uniform – a uniform surely designed to send shivers down a girl's spine.

A friend of my father's, who was travelling on a London bus over Waterloo Bridge, espied this extraordinary little band of people striding out in single column across the bridge, and couldn't resist telephoning my father that evening to ask him what exactly he had been doing earlier that day!

The first call they made was to the United States Army Headquarters, where he asked to see someone high in authority – preferably a General. After waiting for sometime a secretary appeared saying, 'The General will see you now. Will you follow me Major?' They shook hands and my father said to him, 'General, I have come to see you to ask you a favour. My young daughter is going to marry one of your soldiers. I don't know whether you are a family man, but he tells me that he had been given two days off for a honeymoon. Now this young man has fought bravely with General Patton's 3rd Armoured Division, no doubt going through hell, so I am here to see if you can move mountains and get the chap a week's extension, so that they can really have a decent honeymoon. She has only seen him for three or four days since their first meeting, and he has been in Europe for a year.' There was a pregnant pause, then the General's face creased into a broad smile and rising to his feet he said, 'I like that Major, why you British always have such a nice way of putting a case – how could I refuse?' There and then he wrote Hugh out a pass giving him ten days' leave. When my father rejoined them to relate the good news they were overjoyed.

The next call they had to make was to Doctors Commons to obtain the necessary licence. This had to be signed by both parents and as my father had suspected this to be the case, he had purposely brought Enid along, so that she could dash back to my mother's bedside, get her signature and return to London post-haste.

With this section of the arrangements completed, they then all trooped off to the American Rainbow Club in Shaftesbury Avenue, where apart from a much needed bottle of coca cola – a drink that my father had never heard of, let alone tasted – Hugh was anxious to arrange honeymoon accommodation. Whilst Hugh left them in the bar my father found himself surrounded by friendly GIs – it was the one and only occasion he had met them en masse and he told us that he found the experience thoroughly enjoyable.

Hugh came back to forlornly announce that there was no hotel accommodation to be found anywhere. Before they had time to be cast down, however, they became aware that a kindly looking lady was heading in their direction. 'Corporal Smith,' she said smiling, 'You can have the accommodation that I booked for my own one week's leave, which has just this minute been cancelled as we are so busy and they can't spare me – I don't know if it will interest you?' In a flash their faces lit up and without a moments hesitation they accepted this kind lady's offer.

Whilst my father was in London making plans, I had been delegated to make contact by telephone with all the guests that were to be invited to the wedding – which was to be held the day after tomorrow! It was all so sudden. Many of the invitees had attended little Margaret's first birthday party only ten days previously and no mention had been made then of this forthcoming marriage. As you can imagine the phone calls were lengthy, for I had a lot of explaining to do. 'No, we didn't mention it then because we had no idea that Hugh was about to arrive home intent upon marrying Audrey!' The telephone bill must have been colossal that month!

We then had to hurriedly buy Audrey a trousseau. We could have wept (and indeed secretly did) to see my mother lying in her bed with every sinew atwitching, unable to do anything about it – it must have been heartbreaking for her, for Audrey was her special girl and together they had surmounted her illness. It didn't help that I was tied to the house with a toddler. Our very good neighbour and friend, Mrs Weatherill, came down to visit my mother. Putting her hand warmly on my mother's she looked at her and said, 'My dear, I can never take your place at a time like this, but I really would like to help in anyway I can – so I suggest that I take Audrey to London and we scoot around and get her fixed up with a trousseau. So, I don't want you to worry – when we get back Audrey will be able to try on everything in front of you and you can see what we have bought.' She bent over and kissed my mother and left her room hastily, for she didn't want my mother to know that she had noticed big warm tears rolling down her cheeks, and she was on the verge of weeping herself.

My mother was never to see Hugh again. After their wedding and honeymoon he returned to Germany and was then sent home to the USA from there to be demobilised, leaving Audrey at home, lonely and longing to be with her husband. Sadly too, my mother was unable to watch her daughter's wedding, which took place at Christ Church in Guildford.

Audrey looked as pretty as a picture. The dress she and Mrs Weatherill had chosen came from Liberty's and was beautiful. Her pretty wavy dark hair wisped around her face as though it was laughing with Audrey. She chose her childhood friend June as bridesmaid along with a little girl and her brother, whose mother Audrey had been bridesmaid to when she was nine years old. Audrey and Hugh had their wedding reception in the garden at Warren Farm House – a glorious day in June, before they finally departed for their honeymoon in Sussex.

George had by this time transferred from the RAF to the Royal Canadian Airforce, the only bonus as I saw it was to get me transported back to Canada at their Government's expense. So once again we were to be parted, but really parted – this time for nine whole beastly months. With the war on partings had to be expected, and indeed tolerated, but in peacetime and after many lengthy separations, the prospect was just too awful to think about.

My mother had made a reasonable recovery from her last stroke and was up and about again. George had received the news that he was due to sail to Canada in August 1945 and our second wedding anniversary was on 14 August – we had a tearful parting. I remember returning on the train to Guildford from Bournemouth crying unashamedly. The passengers were compassionate for they no doubt had their own experiences of sad partings. That was the marvellous thing about the war, it brought out the very best in people – we laughed together, cried together and we suffered together, rather like one enormous and extremely close family. If only this close tie could last forever.

That night we had an excessively heavy rainfall and severe thunderstorms. My father suspected that we could be in for a flood – Heaven forbid I thought, not again, that was the last thing that we needed. I looked at my dearest father, thinking this really shouldn't be happening to you – you have had more than your fair share to cope with. But I was glad at least that I was beside him, for we had always been very close and I did adore him. This time we prepared for the onslaught. My mother and old Aunt Lilah had gone to bed and we had no intention of telling them of our fears. We started by rolling up the Persian rugs and our sleeves, as on this occasion my father was at the helm. We lifted the furniture onto the tables, took books out of bookcases – and shoved all the cats and dogs upstairs out of the way.

Just as we were finishing our preparations – Wham! Crash! In roared the floodwaters. How much could we stand, I asked myself? This surely would be the last straw so far as my mother was concerned. I was drawn to my father with compassion and my heart went out to him. He was such a good man and yet somehow he was being weighed down with these unbearably heavy tragedies. Firstly Audrey's long illness, now my mother's, these awful floods, the war – where on earth would it end? I waded over to him and put my arms around his neck and we both silently wept together. In some strange way it gave us the strength and courage we needed to continue. We worked like beavers all night, together with Flo and Nellie, Bill and his wife.

On this occasion we could retreat to our flat upstairs and this was a godsend. We had made as many preparations as we could but not everything was safe from the floodwater. The thing that upset me most was the devastated wreck of Margaret's lovely high coach-built pram. It was a beauty that my parents had bought her. It had been knocked over onto its side by the force of the water and when we came down the next morning it had filled up with this stinking, sludgy mud – the flood waters having coursed their way through a dairy farm before hitting Warren Farm House.

At daybreak my father phoned the prisoner of war camp on Merrow Downs and asked for help. Italians were sent, and they quickly got the place in some form of order. They were a happy-go-lucky bunch of men and we soon discovered they were delighted to leave their camp and be with an English family. They adored Margaret on sight and as a result made her some lovely toys – including a brightly painted bumble bee that flapped his wings as she pulled it along. They were very talented – they made cigarette lighters out of old aluminium saucepans that really worked and lovely shopping baskets from hedgerow willows.

I recall being loaned a pram for Margaret by Lord Onslow of Clandon Park until I could get the other one completely renovated. It was an offer not to be sneezed at. Called a Millsom, it was regarded as the Rolls Royce of perambulators – used in the main by nannys in Kensington Gardens and no doubt Buckingham Palace! The coach-work was black and highly polished with a navy blue leather lining. In those days one's own two feet were the accepted form of transport and, as I have already mentioned, Guildford is a town of hills and valleys – we lived in a valley off to the side of a long hill. Off on a shopping spree, I dressed Margaret up to the nines, settled her in this resplendent perambulator and we set out to walk the two miles to Guildford town. She always loved an audience, but on the particular day it was M'Lordship's perambulator that received all the complimentary glances. All was well going to Guildford, for it was downhill all the way. I did my shopping and turned this magnificent vehicle in the direction of home, at which point I very quickly decided that this trip was to be my one and only. I struggled to push this heavy monster up the ever increasing hill, it weighed a ton and it seemed that as I puffed and blew taking one step forward, the demon under the wheels was forcing me two paces backwards. The carriage which had seemed so grand I hated now with a purple passion – and by now I was purple with exertion! I couldn't wait to turn into our gateway and coast down our long drive to the valley below, where hopefully, if I made it, I would be able to revive myself with a cup of tea!

The winter evenings began to draw in. How I loved this time of nature's year. To be able to draw the heavy velvet curtains and pull one's chair alongside a welcoming log fire – all our fires burned logs, for they were inglenooks – for me this was sheer bliss.

Nellie would have tea ready, with a plate of hot buttered toast – not much butter and in fact it was most probably wartime margarine with home-made jam, created with a variety of fruits from our orchard. Perhaps, if we were lucky there would be a hostess cake from Canada, this was a rich fruit cake with the top covered in sticky red and green glazed cherries and pecan nuts. I would play with my toddler in front of the fire before putting her to bed. I was sad, however, that her daddy couldn't share in the joy I was experiencing with our first born. My father was aware of my loneliness and he tried so hard to be both a father to me and to Margaret and generally boost my morale.

Audrey's morale on the other hand was on the up and up, for her plans to be in the USA for Christmas seemed to be materialising. She had to spend days in London undergoing medical examinations – with her past history of severe illness they certainly went over her with a fine-tooth comb. She needed a passport and visa and because she was a minor everything once again had to be signed by both parents.

We went shopping for her new winter clothes, with the long years of war our wardrobes desperately needed replenishing. It's silly the things one remembers, but I can see Audrey to this day sitting alongside the window to benefit from the light, mending her silk stockings. Ladder upon wretched ladder – so much so that in the end she had more repairs than the threads of a spider's web. Very often we would wear no stockings at all, but just paint our legs with leg colouring and then draw a fine pencil line up the back of the leg from heel to thigh, to give the appearance of stockings. Although my mother had a good stock of clothing coupons which had been off loaded onto her from the Canadian soldiers, she had parted with a good few for our two weddings and somehow one was always loath to waste them on items such as stockings and handkerchiefs.

We did in fact have to live with the annoyance of clothing coupons and the five shilling limit on meals for several years after the war. The unpleasant word 'utility' crept into everyday usage – from clothes to furniture. I think that possibly it was the teenagers and young women who found it the most frustrating – not to be able to go out on a whim and buy a dress, a pair of stockings or a silk nightie, for we all love to have pretty clothes. We had already had six long years of war and it became so monotonous having to think up new ideas to renovate hand-me-downs. But we did become ingenious – raiding grandmother's lace drawer, simply adding a new belt and buttons or making the most of whatever clothing items came our way – like I had with Donald's bell-bottomed seaman trousers.

Thankfully, my aunt in Canada managed to beat the strict customs laws and she would send us silk stockings hidden between pages of newspapers or magazines, which she would then proceed to roll up tightly like a sausage, and post it off at newspaper rate!

So it was that Audrey and I would set off for London in the search for new clothes full of good cheer and optimism. On our return home, well pleased with our many purchases, we would lay them out on our mother's bed for her to see. It made her so happy at a time when we were all well aware that Audrey's permanent departure for the United States was looming on the horizon.

11

FLYING THE NEST

News came one morning that Audrey had a seat booked on a flight crossing the Atlantic by way of the Northern Polar route. There were to be no other passengers, only a group of pilots and navigators who were trying out this new route – for it must be remembered that crossing the Atlantic by air was not the normal mode of transport in those long ago days.

Again my parents had to give their consent by signing all the necessary papers. My poor father was full of apprehension, for he loved her so much, but Audrey pleaded with him to say yes – so he did. What a parting it was. Audrey on the one hand was ecstatic that at long last she was going to be with her husband – it was now six months since she had seen him – but sad to be leaving her family behind. Our parents, of course, were heartbroken at losing her. She finally arrived into the bosom of her new American family on Christmas Eve.

We were now a sad and depleted little family, aware of the gap left by the loved ones that were missing from our lives. I felt particularly sorry for Diana, who for the greatest part of her young life had only known the war years. She had experienced her home bulging to breaking point with people who had spoiled her outrageously, now it seemed that one by one they were leaving the farm. Her mother was very unwell, meaning that she had to be quiet whenever she was in the house and could not enjoy simple pleasures like having friends to tea, something that we had taken for granted. The result was that she threw all her energies and love upon Margaret and her two horses, quickly becoming an expert horsewoman and show jumper.

It seemed that her lifestyle, through force of circumstance, was not what ours had been. Additionally, of course, we had had our mother at the helm. Diana did not and therefore became a law unto herself. One thing for certain was that Margaret, over the forthcoming years, was to idolise her, for they were after all only ten years apart in age.

That Christmas Diana and I put on a brave face and set about decorating the Christmas tree and the house, which we always did on Christmas Eve. We were a strange gathering for Christmas 1945. To set the scene I will recall who was there; our parents and dear old Aunt Lilah, who seemed to go from strength to strength. There was Uncle Frank, not really an uncle, but an institution – a bachelor who had spent every Christmas with us for longer than I can recall. He, though very old in years, was young at heart, with a shock of white hair and a nose like an over-ripe strawberry. He used to take snuff and Margaret would watch fascinated, unable to take her eyes off his incredible nose. Flo was there with her little girl Diana, just a baby and so adorable. Last but certainly not least was Nellie, mainstay of the family and life and soul of the gathering once Christmas dinner had been formally served. After this the port would be passed around, which, so far as Nellie was concerned, was her signal to take control of the proceedings, resulting in her becoming a giggle a minute. In addition to the 'family' father had driven off in Puffing Billy, down to the town on his annual mission to gather up lonely soldiers.

Christmas that year was miserable for me, not only for the lack of our loved ones but because Margaret had in an instant become very ill with gastroenteritis. She became dehydrated and was running a very high temperature. I was young and inexperienced with children's illnesses, but my mother was able, despite her own ill health, to take over. In her presence I immediately took comfort, for she transformed our bedroom into a mini hospital ward, complete with a thermometer standing in a shrimp paste jar full of thymol disinfectant. The doctor called three times on Christmas Day, so I knew Margaret must be very ill. I remember clearly breaking down and having a good cry after George telephoned to wish us all a Happy Christmas, for it was so obvious that he was having – which after all was perfectly normal – an enjoyable Christmas time. I was full of self pity and at an all time low.

When one is down in the dumps, however, fate can be kind and alter the situation in a most unexpected way. This happened to me just before New Year's Eve when a second cousin of ours from Ceylon appeared on the doorstep. He had been a Japanese prisoner of war for several years and had just recently been released. He had made his way to England where his sister was nursing at St George's hospital in London. We liked each other on sight – he was at a loose end and so was I. He stayed at the farm for a few weeks before returning to London. From then on life became much more fun. There was a group of about six of us who would go to the theatre, or to dine and dance. My parents encouraged it, for they felt it was high time I got out of the house and mixed with people of my own age. My father said when one is young, life is for living and to be enjoyed to the full. The great advantage that I had was being able to leave Margaret in the capable hands of so many willing helpers – there was Flo and Nellie and always, of course, my mother.

During the post-war years many of my mother's Canadian service boys would turn up, sometimes with their wives, to see how my mother was faring and also to refresh their minds and recall memories of the happy times spent at dear old Warren Farm House. Looking back over the years, it is interesting to note that she opened her home to Canadian boys from all walks of life – from doctors and college boys to bus drivers, foresters and farm hands and she never once had an unpleasant experience with any of them. My father would relate how, on the most unexpected occasions, he would be introduced to some Canadian, who would tell him – much to his surprise – that he had slept in my father's bed and, what's more, in his pyjamas! He never met Tiny though!

All this time my father was making efforts to find me a way of getting across to Canada. It seemed an impossibility – shipping was not to be had at any price. Troops were being transported back home to the USA and Canada to be demobilised, along with nurses and doctors. To crown it all there were so few ships. At last he managed to find me an opportunity for passage on a Norwegian freighter, a very small one which only carried six passengers. However, when he approached the Canadian Government on the matter they flatly refused to consider it, for by now I had become a Canadian Citizen and dependent – this meant that they could lay down the law as far as I and my daughter were concerned. They objected to the fact that I would be the only girl on board, and with a toddler. Additionally it would be February when the seas could be exceptionally rough – what, they asked, would happen to the child if her mother was to fall and break her leg? There would be no doctor on board and no one to take care of the child – so that was that, they successfully made my father feel that he was an uncaring twit! Personally, to be able to get to George I would willingly have taken the gamble, but there was nothing for it but to wait patiently for my allotted turn.

This was about the time of the chicken incident. Diana had always killed chickens when they were needed for the pot prior to leaving the farm for boarding school, she was fearless in this respect. Otherwise, if Bill the cowman was around then he always obliged. Thinking back, however, I realised that, to my knowledge, my mother had never killed anything. It occurred to me to wonder why, and then I had my chance to find out. There I was, dressed in my Sunday going-to-meeting dress and coat and wearing a super new pair of light beige suede shoes that my aunt had sent from Canada. I was running late to catch the train for London, when Nellie appeared holding a chicken upside down by it's legs. 'Muriel dear,' she said, 'Before you dash off could you kill this for me, I need to pluck it and get it ready to pop in the oven for tonight's dinner.' 'Oh, Nellie I can't, do I have to? I don't know how to do it for a start and in any case I'm all dressed up ready to dash off to London.' Well, her face fell a mile, which made feel immediately guilty. It seemed I would have to do it. 'Very well,' I said, 'Give it here and I'll have a go.' I took hold of the chicken's neck and, as I thought I had seen Diana do, gave it a severe twist – thinking that would be that.

But nothing doing – the poor thing was squawking and obviously gasping for breath. I felt dreadful, but having started I knew I had to finish her off at all costs. In sheer terror the poor thing had meesed all over my coat and dress, but I cared not at this point, the thought uppermost in my mind was that somehow I had to kill her. Now, one more huge twist, I said to myself. She struggled and to my horror I found that I had split the skin around her neck and blood was gushing everywhere. She managed to jump out of my grasp and then charged around the courtyard at speed. On her third time round I rugby tackled it – slipping on the wet gravel and ending up in a muddy puddle with this poor unfortunate chicken once more in my grasp. 'Fetch a hammer quickly Nellie, I've simply got to put this bird out of it's misery – quick, for heaven's sake.' Nellie was back in a flash and I'm ashamed to say that I bludgeoned it to death – it was all I could do. By this time I was shaking with disgust at my amateur bungling. I cancelled my trip to London for apart from having ruined just about everything I was wearing, I also felt absolutely dreadful about what I had done and continued to feel so for several days afterwards. I could see why my mother hadn't involved herself in this part of farm life. Indeed it was quite some time before I could face the prospect of eating chicken again.

George was becoming impatient at the long delay in getting his wife and daughter across the Atlantic to join him in Canada. He decided, therefore, to plan a visit to England in May to see if he could precipitate some form of action. On hearing the excellent news that George was on his way to see us, excitement and joy flowed back into my, by now, sluggish veins. Nine long lonely months had passed by and how I had missed him. This news wasn't just welcomed by me. It was a tonic for my mother, for she adored George and the thought of seeing him once more really gave her something to look forward to. It was still only early February but who cared – May would soon be here.

The next two months I spent dreaming about George's homecoming. I had great confidence too that he would somehow manage to get us over to Canada. I must admit that secretly I had reservations about going – though of course I wanted to be with George. Certainly a holiday would be nice, but to plan to live there for ever was another matter and quite a difficult one to come to terms with.

Audrey's husband, Hugh, was a one hundred per cent American boy, and it would never have entered his head to live anywhere else but in the USA and preferably his home town. George, on the other hand, seemed to have totally accepted the English way of living long before I met him. He had made a host of friends and I sensed that he had loved his English way of life almost as much as I did. Not that it really would have mattered, we were brought up to believe in those days that a wife followed her husband – no questions asked. I might be British through and through but I would have to make the best of it – my only hope was that I should not let George down by becoming homesick.

A further, and major, concern at this time was for my mother. She had been very upset by Audrey's departure – I had first hand knowledge of the way she had silently sobbed her heart out over her daughter's leaving. Over the intervening months it seemed that little Margaret had filled the gap in her life – she loved her and made much of her, and I feared what effect our departure would have on her well-being.

George telephoned to say he would be arriving by boat at Southampton and would I meet him as he had masses of luggage to get to us. Excitement was at an all time high and it was decided that Puffing Billy and I would set off for the docks. My mother insisted that we spend a couple of days together, just the two of us, 'Darling,' she said, 'Go somewhere nice – before returning to the farm. You've been parted for far too long – you'll need to get to know one another again – we can look after Margaret.'

I didn't need much persuasion – I booked the bridal suite at the Spread Eagle Hotel in Midhurst, Sussex, supposedly one of the many hostelries that Nell Gwynne had stayed in with King Charles. I cleaned Puffing Billy, he was after all welcoming a very special friend home, and the two of us set off for Southampton on a gloriously warm sunny day in May. We arrived without mishap and I waited excitedly on the quay side, in time to watch the ship as she made her way into port. All one could see was a sea of faces high above the crowd waiting on the quay. I, along with everyone in the crowd, searched through the faces trying to spot familiar features. Suddenly my search was complete – George's face came into view and the last nine lonely months faded away.

Finally we made it to each other's side and how wonderful it was to be together again. As we waited on the docks for George's luggage to be unloaded he said 'Darling, I have arrived with enough loot and contraband in my trunks to put me in prison for years to come – somehow I'm just going to have to try and talk my way through customs.' At that moment we noticed a man in custom officer's uniform waving at us, so we made our way over to him. He greeted George like a long lost buddy, shaking him vigorously by the hand and clapping him on the back. George on the other hand was frantically trying to remember where exactly he could have met him! Anyway he played along with this friendly fellow who said, 'George, let's meet up for a drink when I've finished getting this lot through customs – the pub is bang opposite the main exit.' 'A great idea' replied George. As an afterthought this new-found, old buddy of George's said, 'By the way have you got your luggage through yet?' 'Yes, this is mine here.' 'Fine,' said this heaven-sent being, 'I suppose you haven't anything of special value in there have you?' 'No,' lied my husband, 'Just the usual presents.' With which this marvellous fellow put his magic chalk marks on all George's luggage and we parted, arranging to meet later.

Naturally we then loaded everything into Puffing Billy and left the docks as quickly as he would take us – and that was too slow for comfort. George was at a loss to remember where he had met this officer, wherever it was it had paid off for he had done us a marvellously good turn. It was not until several days later that the penny dropped – it hadn't been in an RAF Squadron as George had first thought, but last year in Bournemouth, when he had been sent there to take charge of the airforce servicemen returning to Canada to be demobilised. This man had apparently been the RTO at the embarkation and he and George had been once or twice to a pub for a drink together.

I broke the good news to George that we were to spend a couple of nights away before going home and that I had booked into the Spread Eagle Hotel. Imagine my great disappointment therefore when he quashed the whole idea instantly. 'Darling, that's quite out of the question. I am worried to death that all the food that I have in my trunk will be rancid – there's a whole ham, masses of bacon and a host of other things – you see it's been tightly packed in there for nearly ten days and in this hot weather, well, anything could have happened to it, at all costs I must get it to your mother in a healthy and good smelling state I'm afraid.' I simply couldn't believe it – it was a case of the ham or me and, damn it, the ham had won! From that moment all those years ago, I came to the realisation, as no doubt have many women before and after me – that food takes precedence over all else.

So we made for home and it was as if the prodigal son had arrived back into the family fold. We were all delighted to have him back. But it was the ham which completely stole the show – it became Christmas time in May and fully made up for the rather miserable time we had had less than six months previously. There was sugar, a colossal cheese, cookies – in fact every conceivable kind of food stuff. Also there were clothes for Margaret and me – even shoes and a handbag. It was tremendously exciting and, I must admit, well worth coming straight home for. One item I shall never forget were the high fashion black suede shoes he bought for me. They were ankle strapped, had platform soles with very high heels and the platforms were covered with gold studs. I, naturally, was thrilled to bits with them, but wondered if I'd ever have the nerve to wear them. I must explain why – prostitutes in London, as mentioned earlier, were always the first to wear the latest fashions from the other side of the Atlantic (for obvious reasons) and the very last time I was in London those very stylish shoes were already being worn – on the beat! However, I couldn't hurt George's feelings, so I decided to blazes with it, and we sallied forth to London to dine and dance at the Mayfair Hotel.

We spent a very happy few weeks. George was getting to know his daughter, and me too I suppose. We rode and lazed in the garden. Diana was in her element having George on the farm, and the three of us would go for long rides over the beautiful Surrey Downs. The signs of war had long since gone – the tented army encampments occupied throughout the war years by the Canadian regiments, the endless army vehicles and troop convoys, fighter and bomber planes overhead were now all but a distant nightmare. The only evidence left was the German prisoner of war camp on Merrow Downs – still fully occupied.

On one occasion we were riding on these downs passing the camp. The prisoners lined the wire fences and there were a few shouts and whistles – not bad for our ego I hasten to add. George was riding my father's horse, which took quite a lot of handling and liked to lead the way. As we were galloping along George signalled that we should go straight ahead. Diana and I had other ideas, we planned to turn right along the other side of the prison fence. George's horse, however, on realising that we were not behind him swung round and did a hefty double buck. A thousand prisoners gave a resounding YIPPEE and a colossal cheer as George flew through the air and landed somewhat unceremoniously on his backside. He said afterwards that at that point he could have climbed into that prison and used his horsewhip to beat every God-damned one of them – and then us too! He was not amused, but we certainly were!

We were still having visits on the farm from the Milk Marketing Board, who came regularly to test our milk. On one occasion their representative commented to me 'Your daughter is as pretty as a picture, have you ever thought of having her painted?' 'Yes, many times' I replied, 'but it would be too expensive to contemplate and it's only worth having done if you can afford the best.' 'Well that's not difficult' was his reply. 'If you give me a bar of soap and a packet of cigarettes I can get it done for you by one of the German prisoners up at the camp, he was a well-known portrait painter in Germany before the war – even painted Hitler I've heard tell. If you can give me a photograph, a piece of her hair and details of her eyes and dress – colour etcetera – he will be only too pleased to do it, he told me he was sick to death of painting fellow male prisoners.'

Well I was thrilled at the prospect, I dashed upstairs and found a recent studio photograph of Margaret which we all loved, and cut off one of her curls. I gave it all to the Milk Marketing Board man along with not one but two bars of soap and a whole carton of cigarettes; then sat back in anticipation.

On his next monthly visit the man brought the finished painting in oils. We were speechless, for it was an exact copy of our beautiful photograph. He had mounted the canvas on a wooden frame and had burnt out, as though a living record 'H. FIEDLER. 6.1946' and as a double safeguard had stuck on the back of the canvas the following, most beautifully written in ink: 'Artist. Horst Fiedler – Berlin = Kopenick, Mahlsdorfer Str. 18 – Germany'. We never met him, but how I would have loved to even though one had to remember that they were still the enemy who had recently caused such appalling devastation across the country.

A German colonel friend of ours from Bonn attempted some years ago to track him down, but without success, for at that time the soldier artist lived behind the Berlin wall in East Germany.

Around this time many days were being spent in London trying to find a ship to take us to Canada. We had been led to believe by the Canadian Government that we would be allowed to travel together, but that was not to be and once again we were to face disappointment and separation. George had to sail two weeks ahead of us, Margaret and I had been given, at long last, a booking on the *Queen Mary*, to sail on the 10 July 1946. She was still being used as a troop ship and was kitted out as such, the cabins were lined with bunk beds and all in all it was rather Spartan. We were told that approximately 500 of us, with our children, would be on this crossing along with returning servicemen, doctors and nurses. Our official definition on board was to be 'Canadian dependants'.

Just before George sailed we took his beloved bitch Havoc to Kent where a wartime Air Force friend of George's had offered to give her a home. What should have been a pleasant weekend visit turned out to be the most tear-jerking occasion. I can't put my finger on it exactly, but deep down I was far from happy about leaving Havoc there – I have always had a kind of intuition and I certainly feared something was wrong then. My father had said to George to mention to his friend that if for some reason he found that he could no longer keep Havoc, then to let him know and he would like to have her back on the farm. As we drove away on the Sunday afternoon, dear old Havoc broke out of their garden and ran alongside our car, as though saying, 'Hey, wait for me George.' We had to turn round and drive her back, which was heartbreaking for me – I dared not look at George, he was nutty about that dog, they really had become inseparable over the years. It also reminded me that I had to face up to being parted from my dear Judy within the next two weeks. If only, I thought, one could talk to them and tell them that they would be well cared for and loved by somebody else.

As it turned out, on our return to England the following year, George telephoned his friend to tell him we were back home again, only to be told that he had had to have Havoc put to sleep, because he had been divorced and couldn't cope with a dog. We were utterly shocked and realised that Havoc should have stayed at Warren Farm House after all.

12

CANADA BOUND

The two weeks between seeing George off and Margaret and I leaving were hectic. All of our goods and chattels had to be crated up into large wooden boxes. We had all Margaret's toys – her doll's pram and tricycle – and our wedding presents and a few antiques that we had acquired, but we had no furniture as such. There were endless forms to be filled in, and bills to be paid – and of course farewells to be said. My heart was heavy in so many ways, for I was parting with the very things that I had loved for so much of my life. Dear Stjarni and my mare Sally – I just couldn't visualise life without our animals and, of course, dear old Warren Farm House itself.

I had come to the conclusion that once we departed, the farm would be a house without a soul. We had all been together for so long, through thick and thin. In many ways I felt I was deserting them all. I went down to say goodbye to Diana at her school in Dorset and we had a quick tear together. Then there were all of our dogs, dear old Pluto to whom we owed so much and Judy. I couldn't look at my Judy I felt so miserable.

My mother was distraught, and clung to me begging me not to leave her and take Margaret away from her. I was pretty mixed up by it all – Mother would never have given way like this in her strong days. Really this should have been a happy time, starting a new life with my husband. Yet, along with everyone else, I was as unhappy and miserable as could be – our departure had become the cause of so much sadness.

It was in this vein, my mind not concentrating on the job in hand, that I managed to knock out my top front teeth! On the morning before we were due to leave the farm, when making Margaret's dropside cot, I brought the side of the cot up with a sudden jerk without realising that my face was so close — bang, I hit my mouth severely on the bars of her cot. I felt a peculiar crunch and upon investigation I discovered to my horror that I had knocked my three front teeth up into the roof of my mouth. I was appalled — what on earth was I going to do at this late stage, with all the last minute preparations to attend to.

Standing in front of the mirror I gingerly got hold of the teeth and tried to lower them back into position — they were, thank heaven, still attached, albeit loosely. By the time the numbness had worn off though the pain was fearful — and the teeth were really flapping.

My mother took one look at me and insisted that I went at once up to London to our dentist. It was all such a futile waste of precious time, but I knew that I had to go — it was by now quite obvious that they were never going to tighten up of their own accord. The dentist cast his experienced eye over them and said, 'Muriel — no way can I do anything about fixing your teeth, you say you are leaving tomorrow and to extract them and make you a plate would be impossible, with all the will in the world. Now I suggest that I brace them up with fine wire — to form a kind of splint, then at least your front teeth will be in position, remember that far worse things have happened at sea!'

What a sight I looked when I arrived back home. My mouth was swollen and black and blue. My front teeth were lashed together with four bands of wire — not a pretty sight. The thought of having to arrive in Canada to meet all my new relatives looking like this was quite appalling — really, what a fool I'd been. Well, I thought, they will just have to accept me as I am — at least I'll be different. Cold comfort but very true.

Our instructions from the Canadian Government were that we had to present ourselves at a London address in Bayswater, where we would be rounded up (like a flock of sheep perhaps?), counted and generally sorted out. We had to take an overnight bag with our night clothes and a change of clothes for one day for our children, also a packet of sandwiches and milk for drinking. My mother had bought me a very snappy white zipper bag – not very large, but large enough to accommodate these requirements. My father arranged for Nellie to travel up with us to London so that she could help us find the address at which we were to meet up.

All our crates and luggage had to be clearly marked and stored in the hold of the ship and the luggage we needed for the journey we had to clearly label 'To go to the cabin'. My father planned to meet our train at Waterloo and see to the luggage. Flo was to remain with my mother.

To this day I cannot bring myself to recall that heartbreaking parting – we all gave way completely to our emotions. There was, however, no other way. Indeed had my mother not done the self-same thing to her mother, all those years ago, when as a young nurse she had left the bosom of her family to go they knew not where. It seemed that history was repeating itself and I was at a loss to know how best to cope with it. Little did I realise that by the time I had crossed the Atlantic and reached Montreal, I was to have second thoughts about ever having decided to come to Canada, such was our journey.

We arrived by taxi at the address in Bayswater and yet again had to go through a round of farewells. Farewell to my beloved father whose love and attention, for all his children, had been never ending. 'Goodbye Daddy darling.' I hugged him tightly and he then lifted Margaret up into his arms, tears unashamedly rolling down his cheeks. 'Bye, bye Grandpa' Margaret said giving him a big kiss, then I dived into the building not daring to look back. I had said goodbye to Nellie at Waterloo, for I explained to her that the final parting with my father was going to have to be quick as my emotions were strained to breaking point.

We reported to the desk, names were taken and we were shown into a vast dormitory, crammed full of triple tier bunk beds. The noise was deafening, kids screaming, others rushing around the beds, mothers shrieking and bawling after them to come back. It was a chaotic scene and I was loath to become part of it.

We had to queue to get a cup of tea and there appeared to be a total lack of organisation. We were not allowed to leave the room, I kept glancing at myself in the mirror and the sight that stared back at me was about as ghastly as the surroundings. All I wished for was to get into bed and have done with this day. Being summer, the nights were late in coming and as we had no curtains at the huge windows, it was impossible to get the children to sleep. I took Margaret into my bunk with me and we cuddled up together – out of sheer emotional exhaustion we finally drifted off into a restless sleep.

The day started at dawn, because the light wakened up all the children and the noise and the clatter began all over again. We had been told to be ready to leave the hostel at nine in the morning to go to Waterloo in coaches to catch the boat train for Southampton. It was an excessively hot day, the carriages were unbearably stuffy and there were of course the normal delays which turned a comparatively short journey into a tedious and rather slow one.

We were told to eat the sandwiches that we had brought with us for lunch on the train. Can you imagine my horror when I unzipped my nice white bag to find that the milk thermos had tipped over and leaked all over everything. The milk had turned sour – no doubt due to the heat and horror upon horrors, everything had turned bright orange! Investigating further, I discovered a piece of orange cardboard had been fitted into the bottom of the bag and this was now sodden with sour milk. Margaret's pretty new silk dress was orange and smelling to high heaven. I quickly zipped the bag up again and hid it under the seat. No lunch for us that day, which was hard to try and explain to Margaret, who by this time was not only hungry but very thirsty.

We eventually arrived at Southampton and the *Queen Mary* – a beautiful ship. She already seemed to be seething with people, in a way it was as though a small town had decided to go to sea, such was the activity on board.

To set the scene you must imagine that there were 500 of us
– from all walks of life – all going to join our husbands. The ages
seemed to vary enormously from young women like myself to middle aged women who had married for the second time around – and
a massive number in between. There were babes in arms, toddlers,
boys and girls and teenagers. We were to spend five days together
under somewhat cramped conditions and it was certainly to be the
survival of the fittest, or perhaps I should say toughest, for one certainly needed to be tough and thick skinned to survive under these
conditions!

Like sheep, we were once again herded into a long queue – the
idea being to report to the purser's office to be allocated our cabins.
This took about an hour, a tedious wait in a very stuffy passageway.
I at last found my cabin – it was a nice one on 'A' deck with two
portholes, making it light and airy. Very quickly I was joined by two
Cockney girls with babes in arms, who had obviously struck up a
friendship. They took one look at me and said 'Hope your brat isn't
going to natter all night and keep us and the babies awake.' A nice
friendly greeting, I thought; I can't say I was ecstatic about spending five days in their company either. The babies started bawling, so
there and then I decided to go to the purser's office to see if I could
change my cabin.

It involved another long wait, during which an officer called out
my name on the loud speaker, along with others, and told us to
report to the purser. Well, here I was in the queue already. They gave
me the depressing news that our particular cabin baggage had been
packed in the hold, and they would be unable to get it out for us.
Charming, I thought – now what do we do? Five days is a mighty
long time to exist without a change of clothes or shoes – all we had
was what we stood up in. It was a real blow – I had really gone to
town kitting ourselves out with pretty new clothes for the trip. We
had a nightie each, though these would have to be washed because
of the dye and sour milk, but we had no slippers or dressing gowns,
no books or toys for the journey and precious little makeup, for that

was all in my beauty case down in the hold. I could have wept, but come to think of it I had no tears left to shed, for they had all dried up too.

As I stood pondering the situation I began chatting to a lady with a quaint little daughter aged about four and named Rebecca. She was telling me that her cabin mates were ghastly, and she was queuing to see if she could possibly change her cabin. I told her I was doing exactly the same, and so we decided to go it together. Eventually our turn came and the purser said yes to our request, but unfortunately the new accommodation was an inside cabin situated on 'E' deck. To find it we had to go down and down through the ship – to the point where we were fully expecting to find ourselves in the engine room, certainly if the clanking and throbbing were anything to go by. We opened the door of the cabin and to our amazement found four other people already in there, one of whom was a ten-year-old boy, who turned out to be every bit as naughty as Richmal Crompton's *Just William*.

The washbasin and loo led off the cabin and the bunk beds hugged the walls. The air was stifling – no port hole – and there was precious little room. It was obvious that we were going to have to dress by numbers, if we'd ever manage to get dressed at all, with this wretched boy who seemed to have eyes in the back of his head. He had a habit of standing like an idiot in the middle of the small cabin, picking his nose.

While my new-found friend and I were assessing the scene, an officer came in to say that there were four meal sittings at regular intervals. Breakfast to be served from 7.15 a.m. to 9.30 a.m. and dinner from 6 p.m. to 8.15 p.m. I waited to see what the mother and her ten-year-old son were going to choose, for if we went at another time, we stood a chance of having the cabin to ourselves, to take a shower in comfort. Also, by going to different sittings either I or my new friend could keep an eye on our daughters – for no way would we ever have left them with this little stinker playing tricks in the cabin. She luckily chose the first sitting, which suited us well – we

then chose the third and fourth. The children would then hopefully be ready for their sleep and would drop off without further
ado. I had devised a sort of bed harness out of plaited string that a
sailor managed to find for me, I was so worried that Margaret might
wander out of the cabin and goodness knows where she might have
ended up.

I had chosen to travel in a rather snappy new suit that I had had
made with the forthcoming journey in mind. The tailor had made a
pair of trousers in the same lovely worsted material. His shop was in
Conduit Street, London, and he had really gone to town, but then
so he should have, for he had made all my WAAF Officer uniforms
during the war. With the misplacement of my luggage, this suit was
all I had to wear for the entire journey. My shoes, to go with the suit,
were navy with white buckskin and were called 'spectators' – after
three days of wearing them constantly, however, they became navy
and black!

I slept in my pants and bra as my nightie had been ruined with the
orange dye. My main prayer was that my one and only pair of stockings would not ladder, for I had no more to rely on. Margaret's dress
I washed out each night and then I used to queue to use the iron,
sometimes I had to queue for well over an hour. In the end I became
wise, waited until midnight and found there to be no queue at all!

I virtually walked the Atlantic, for Margaret was an extremely active
child and I didn't dare let her out of my sight for one moment. I would
enviously look at other mums lounging in deck chairs with a sleepy
child sucking its thumb, seemingly content to pass away the hours.
Margaret's problem no doubt stemmed from the fact that she was
always having to run as fast as her little legs would carry her, just to keep
up with her Aunty Diana – whom she idolised. It was as though she
had ants in her pants, for whenever I cuddled her onto my lap to read
her a story, she would stretch and slide off saying, 'Down Mummy, get
down!'

There were many officers and troops returning to their homeland,
and they would chat to Margaret (possibly as a way of chatting me

up) and on occasion would ask me if they could borrow her to take her off to their cabins to fetch her a Hershey chocolate bar and to show her off to their friends. I would agree readily and make for a deck chair as fast as my legs would take me, collapse into it and rev up my batteries before her return, to be ready to once again set off at a cracking pace around the deck. It was on one such promenade that I bumped into the ship's doctor, who was a delightful chap. He began by admiring Margaret and then noticed all the barbed wire fencing across my top front teeth. 'What has happened may I ask to your teeth?' he said. 'You may well ask,' I replied. 'I had a particularly stupid accident the day before we had to report to the hostel in London.' I told him the whole miserable story and I think he felt sorry for me. He invited me to join him for dinner in the officer's mess that evening, which was super, for our dining hall was positively revolting. It was arranged that I would go to his surgery and he would attempt to try and make a neater job of my wire brace – the sharp ends of which were by now digging into my inner lip.

Let me tell you about our dining hall for, as I mentioned earlier, we had four separate sittings. The tables and chairs were never wiped clean after each sitting, so bits of food – soggy cornflakes, spilt orange juice, apple and orange peel or milk lay swilling around everywhere. Why, my mother's pigswill was collected in a far cleaner and more hygienic state. We even had to battle with vomit and it seemed the more we complained the less interested the staff became. If you wanted to be put off your food, then there was no more successful way than to cast your eyes over this messy sight.

I told my cabin mate that I had been invited out to have dinner with the ship's doctor – Harry McNicoll from Hamilton – and she quickly volunteered to put Margaret to bed and stay with both our little girls, for we had decided by this time that the boy in the cabin was the devil incarnate. The following night my friend had been invited out to dine in the mess with an officer who was returning home and who was in her husband's regiment, so I was able to return the favour.

I always have to smile when I think of Rebecca, she was an old fashioned little girl, who had big dreamy eyes staring out of a pale pointed little face. She chewed her fingernails and as a result had to wear woollen gloves all the time, no matter how hot the weather – I often wondered if it did the trick! She had a tiny little doll's suitcase that she took everywhere. I seem to recall that their name was Clarke. It is hard to imagine her now – she must be nudging fifty.

I spent an enjoyable evening with the doctor and felt human once more, for their dining room was sumptuous. I felt incredibly scruffy, for I was still in the same, by now weary, suit it seemed to have lost its snappiness and here it was only the second day out to sea. Three more days to go – what on earth would I look like by then? And that wasn't the end of the journey by a long chalk, we had to spend a further two days on a train from Halifax to Montreal.

The divisions on the ship between the returning officers and the Canadian dependants – or war brides as we came to be known – were very obvious. We were classed with the troopers and at every turn one came face to face with a large authoritative sign saying 'Out of bounds to Canadian dependants' it certainly made one feel a third class citizen. We had been told in information pamphlets that we had received before leaving Britain that the VADs on board were there to help dependants with their children. This in fact turned out to be a load of codswallop – VADs were there in abundance, but they had no intention of even helping each other – let alone we war brides! The atmosphere on the ship was one of great excitement, for them especially, for they were returning home at long last, to see their families, to pick up the familiar threads of their lives again. The war was over and Canada was on the horizon waiting to welcome them home again.

For us on the other hand there was an atmosphere of anticipation and excitement, but also fear of the unknown. We were not returning home to a hero's welcome, for we had left all that was very dear and familiar to us behind.

We needed the help of these VADs – some of us more desperately so than others. I was fine on that count, for my cabin mate and I were able to help each other but there were mothers on board with babies as well as toddlers, who were being appallingly seasick. The smell was putrid and the sight of it utterly disgusting. We all tried to help where we could, but it wasn't enough — anyone who has ever suffered seasickness would understand.

Love affairs or final flings were commonplace, and the tannoy system worked overtime calling to one mother or another to go back to her cabin, 'Your child is screaming' or 'Has fallen out of the top bunk' or, as I remember with horror on one occasion 'Mrs Bloggs your child is hanging over the rails on the sundeck!' It was obvious that nature being what it is, the VADs and nurses were having monumental final flings and some of the war brides too. An attachment at sea after all is so romantic, what with the water, the throbbing engines, the music wafting as though through a gauzy veil and dear old Mr Moon casting his silver beams across the waters. Eros could certainly be accused of playing his old tricks on that hot summer crossing. After all, why not? No one was going to tell tales, so how could anyone be hurt? Once the ship docked everyone would be going their separate ways and memories of life on board ship would be locked away in one's own treasure chest, perhaps to be taken out and re-lived in the twilight years.

After a delightful evening of dining and dancing I returned to my cabin. My friend was still up and about and signalled that she wanted to talk to me, so we slipped outside the cabin. 'Muriel' she said, 'both girls have been dreadfully sick and have got diarrhoea – I know you don't have any clothes for Margaret, so I have put a pair of Rebecca's pants on her, but I am at a loss to know just what we can do.' 'We'll take them as soon as we can in the morning to the sick bay' I said. Luckily, because of my friendship with the doctor, we were seen, rather unfairly, straight away. But I was brought up by a father who always preached to us that it is who you know, not what you know, that really counts in life and in this case he was right.

They both had severe gastroenteritis and we were told to keep them in bed, which meant that we were virtually prisoners way down below decks in our cabin. We would run a shuttle service up to the dining room to grab something to eat. I was given great rolls of cotton wool and cotton gauze to pin around Margaret, and her sole pair of pants were washed several times a day. At this time it was announced on the tannoy that an epidemic of polio had broken out on board ship as well as enteritis and measles. This was not surprising when one thought about the germ-infested state of the dining hall and public rooms – when one thought about it, 500 people represented the size of a village in Britain and we were all living in confined conditions.

The announcement about polio sent a chill down our spines, for there was nothing anyone could do about that, it was a fearful disease, more so due to our lack of knowledge about it, though we knew the end results were horrendous – there were reminders in every town in Britain. The warning continued, advising us not to sunbathe for more than five to ten minutes in any one day and to limit our fruit intake. You may well ask about the latter – quite simply we had been deprived of fruit now for nearly six years and to see before our eyes great baskets of Canadian peaches the size of a small melon, to be able to sink one's teeth into the soft flesh with the juice bursting out was sheer bliss. One was followed by two, was followed by three and the end results were obviously disastrous. I recall two girls being taken off the ship on stretchers when the ship docked, and rushed to hospital with severe sunstroke and burns. I felt at the time that this was awful for their small toddlers, who were crying miserably as they were taken into the care of a strange Red Cross lady, having to watch the one and only person familiar to them being taken away.

Rebecca and Margaret were still very sick, it is amazing how quickly little children can go downhill – at this point the main difference between them was that Rebecca had plenty of changes of clothes, underwear in particular, whereas Margaret had none. I smelled like a polecat, for she had constantly been sick over me, and I felt I must by now be the most unsavoury woman on board ship!

Our last day on board was spent queuing to have an interview with the RTO (the railway transport officer), to check our final destinations.

My turn came at long last. He looked up and asked my name. He then said 'Ah! Yes, Mrs Pushman, you are going to Ottawa, that's fine.' 'But sir,' I said, 'I'm not, in fact my husband is meeting me in Toronto, he has filled in the necessary forms to that effect.' The officer looked at his papers again and then back at me. More firmly he said, 'I'm sorry Mrs Pushman, but my papers say Ottawa, so to Ottawa you must go.' I was holding Margaret in my arms, who was limp with illness and I was so exhausted, my clothes were a mess, I was a mess and we must have looked a sorry sight. I snapped at him 'But this is quite ridiculous, my husband is in Toronto, and I have no one to meet me in Ottawa, and certainly will have nowhere to go.' The fact that all my husband's relations were there never entered my weary head. So far as my geography was concerned, Ottawa could have been as far away from Toronto as Timbuktoo.

I was now very close to tears, but fate was being kind to me, because suddenly my nice doctor friend appeared before me, 'Muriel, I've been looking everywhere for you, to say goodbye and to give Margaret a final check over.' Seeing that I was having problems he stepped in to take control. 'Now, what is the problem RTO?' He very quickly became angry with this officious little man and raising his voice he stated, 'If Mrs Pushman says that her husband is waiting for her in Toronto, then to Toronto she must go, she has a very sick little girl, and all this ridiculous red tape isn't helping anybody.' From that moment on I was magically taken care of. I went to the surgery and he gave me some more medicine for Margaret, lots more wadding and a few comforting words. He felt, he said, certain that she would take a turn for the better within the next twenty-four hours. We bade each other farewell and I thanked him for all his concern and kindness, indeed I shall always remember him for it.

I said my farewells to Rebecca and her mother; we had formed quite a bond having gone through a lot of worry together in these past five days. All we had to do now was to wait patiently to leave the *Queen Mary* and embark on the trains.

Whilst waiting I was intrigued to watch the inhabitants of Halifax, who had come down the quayside in their hundreds to view the incoming brides from Britain. It was almost as though they were at a cattle market sizing up the goods. I suspect that many were far from happy that their boys had abandoned Canadian girls for this lot and I must admit that, after this close encounter trip, they had my sympathy to some extent.

Halifax I thought was a beautiful harbour, rather like Loch Inver in Scotland on the north-west coast. It was surrounded by pine tree clad hills, little clapboard – or to we British, wooden, houses and red-roofed barns. The soil was rich sandy colour deepening to terra-cotta. It was, I recall, horse-shoe shaped and the *Queen Mary* seemed to take up the entire harbour. The sun was shining brightly in a clear blue sky. At long last the gangways were down, and we were slowly herded towards the station alongside the quay where the trains were waiting to take us to our various destinations, rather like the spokes of a vast wheel, to start our new lives in this large and unfamiliar country called Canada.

We had each been given a piece of paper with our coach and carriage numbers plainly printed on it, so there could be no mistake. I found my allotted space with no difficulty, all I longed for now was to be able to put my limp little bundle down somewhere – anywhere. Two days on a train I thought would be bliss – just to sit for two whole days and gather myself together once more.

But my thoughts of bliss were soon to be shattered when we were to discover just what conditions were in store for us. The grumbling began in a matter of minutes and could be heard throughout the train, increasing in volume and irate language as it rolled forward from carriage to carriage. Cattle would have been given better treatment, we felt it was an insult to human beings and we were by now all very angry indeed and fed up to the back teeth with the Canadian Government.

The trains were made up of pre-war rolling stock. I was to sleep on an upper bunk bed with Margaret and one other complete stranger – despite the fact that we had all been on the ship together, I cannot ever remember seeing any of these mothers before. In any case, we should never have been expected to sleep in an overcrowded bunk with a total stranger. Even during the height of the Blitz in London, when people were sleeping on mattresses on the platforms of the underground stations, families had privacy and the opportunity to make their own sleeping arrangements.

As we sat in a semi stupour, in came a coloured sleeping car attendant, who announced 'I's come to pull down your bunks missus'. With a half baked grin stretching from ear to ear, before we knew it, he had pulled down the bunks from the walls, dropped the curtains, and shuffled out. 'Well, this is bloody daft, we can't squat like this all effing night' was the comment of my companion, whereupon she took a drag on her fag. I looked at my travelling mate without so much as batting an eyelid, though I hadn't heard that incredible word since I'd left the WAAF. Oh well, why should I worry I thought to myself? Obviously her children are used to it and mine is too young to pick it up. 'There's not a lot we can do about it,' I replied. It feel as though we were in some Middle Eastern bridal tent with all those wretched curtains hanging down, it made it unbearably hot and sticky and we had the whole evening ahead of us to look forward to being crouched uncomfortably.

Margaret was being sick again. I rushed her at top speed in the direction of the toilet doing my utmost to cover up her mouth with a wodge of cotton wool – the only thing I had masses of, thanks to the ship's doctor. But to my dismay I found a long queue ahead of me – with mothers in the same predicament as I and, as we had no containers, the obvious happened all along the corridor.

At this point the train had pulled into a station and we all made a frantic dash to offload in more ways than one onto the station platform. Imagine our embarrassment at having to do this in our new country, we felt our behaviour was very ill bred, but we had no option.

We clambered back onto the train which was so humid and stifling – more so for us as we had never experienced this kind of excessive heat in Britain. We pulled all the windows down to their fullest extent, not realising that we were near the front of the train and the steam engine. Therefore, in a trice, we were covered from head to foot in greasy, sooty smuts – in some ways it was worth it just to hear my companion get herself really worked up. 'Gaw, luv a duck, I'm gonna murder the bloody jerk who thought this one up – the effing boat was a piss hole, but this – gaw blimey.' I dived in behind my curtains, for it was all I could do to keep a straight face.

Two dramatic incidents happened on that journey – we ran out of water within the first three hours and the loos became completely blocked. I could not imagine two more essential facilities for any human being, never mind a train transporting all these women with their babies and children. The girls with young babies on bottles became demented and one could hear them dashing up and down the corridors trying to find someone in authority, for they were by now hysterical. 'We must have water – boiling water to make up the milk and then to sterilise the bottles' they cried. They had been reduced to tears – understandably so.

The loos were overflowing with the blockages and the resulting smells in the hot weather were putrid. On this occasion I had absolutely no intention of offering my expert services to try and unblock them, even though I had, during my time in the WAAF, become an expert toilet cleaner and unblocker!

Word got around the next morning that a deputation had stormed up the train, found the RTO and demanded that he had the train stopped at the very next station in order to resolve the two main problems. He was requested to arrange for freshly boiled water to be on tap for the rest of the journey and to make available facilities for sterilising the babies bottles.

When the train did finally stop we too joined the bandwagon, demanding that our windows be oiled, so that we could open and close them when we wished to. By now the damage had already been done and we were quite as black as the sleeping car attendant. It was said that the RTO was by this time so terrified of these furious British women that he carried out all their demands to the full.

What perhaps he and most Canadians didn't fully appreciate was the fact that we had spent six years under the most appalling tensions. Our fuses were therefore short – particularly when we came face to face with bungling bureaucracy.

There always has to be a silver lining and for me it was arriving in Quebec City at midnight. By this time I had shinned up onto my top bunk, where I was wedged in like a sardine between Margaret and one of the daughters of my Cockney friend – who by this time was snoring her head off down below us. I was aware of a lot of clanging of chains and a great deal of French chatter amongst the dockers. I pulled the blind back, and the sight before my eyes was one of fairy wonderland – an enchanted city. We were just passing underneath the bridge and the city lay stretched out before us in the midnight sky – liberally scattered with stars. The city itself was lit up like a giant Christmas tree and I watched spellbound. It must be recalled that in Britain street and shop lighting were not permitted until June 1949.

The last day on the train was spent making the most of a bad job – trying to smarten up Margaret and myself. I was envious of all the other girls changing into the special outfits they had bought to meet their husbands in. Here was I, still in the now sick-stained suit that I had worn to travel to Southampton, my shoes were dirty and my stockings laddered. Margaret was in much the same state – making us a pathetic pair. With all the travellers finally going their separate ways it had finally dawned on us that the last threads of our ties to Britain were soon about to be snapped and we would be on our own, ready to forge a new way of life in Canada.

As we headed towards Montreal the pompous little RTO man came along the train to see me to say, 'Mrs Pushman, when we arrive at Montreal you will have to make your own way across the city to the other station.' It was obvious I thought, that in his eyes I should be going to Ottawa. 'Now, you will have to hurry for there is only just sufficient time to make the connection.' I gathered up my mea-gre belongings, for I had long since given up worrying about my luggage and where it could be – or when, if ever, I would see it again. For all I knew it could still be in the hold of the *Queen Mary* heading back to England!

Slowly the train came to a grinding halt – Montreal, here we are. What a relief to know there was no more government-organised travelling in store. I made a stir to get out as I had been instructed to, when an official of some kind followed by two ladies in uniform stepped onto the train and into our carriage. 'Now ladies, will you please all remain in your seats until otherwise told to move.' Feeling like a schoolgirl I put up my hand, 'Please – I have to catch a connection to Toronto from your other station in Montreal and I am only just going to be able to make it.' The official looked at me, smiled a watery kind of smile and said 'Now dear, do try to be patient like everybody else, we know you are anxious to meet your dear ones, but I am afraid on this occasion you will just have to abide by the rules.' I sunk back on my seat, closed my eyes and tried to blot out my anger. I had to accept the fact that I would miss my connection – I just hoped there will would be others.

The reason for keeping us all boxed up on the train was explained to us later. It was in fact to safeguard us. The husbands were gathered together on the station, almost herded like sheep in a pen. This had over the months become necessary, because so many husbands just never turned up to claim their British wives and children, for a variety of reasons, including the fact that some had already married before they had come overseas to fight in the war. Others, it was said, lived on Red Indian reserves and some were even known to have spun yarns to their wives in Britain that they were landowners, or farmers, when in fact they were nothing of the sort and invariably hadn't had a job in years. This situation would leave a pathetic wife and her little family standing on the station with no one to meet them and claim them – which sadly meant they had to be returned home to Britain.

The new system was for the husband's name to be called out whereupon he would step forward, if he was there, and his wife and family would be released from the train to join him. I tried to explain that I hadn't in fact got a husband meeting me in Montreal. 'He is in Toronto, that is why I should have caught that connection, so that we could have joined him there tonight' I said somewhat sourly, but to little avail. I had visions of being shipped back to Britain and in my present mood I would have jumped at the idea – even if it did mean wearing this smelly old suit for several days longer!

Looking out of the train window for want of something better to do, I espied a dapper little man walking at great speed along the platform, accompanied by two Red Cross ladies. His smart appearance intrigued me – in London I knew that stationmasters dressed like that – could he be the local stationmaster I wondered? Imagine my amazement when the two ladies brought him right up to me. My mind started to work overtime, I knew that he could not possibly be my father-in-law, for he had a gammy leg, and I didn't imagine him to be any of my brothers-in-law either.

He was neither – with a broad smile he said 'How do you do, you must be Muriel? I am Charles Coyle, a friend of your husband's, George is desperate with worry and he telephoned me and asked me to come and rescue you from this train – I've had quite a time I can tell you trying to break through all the red tape.' 'How very kind' I said smiling back at him, 'I can assure you that to say goodbye to this train will be an enormous relief.' He was a kindly man and very jolly. We were driven back to his sumptuous apartment, where there were two charming ladies and their elderly mother waiting to shower kindness upon us.

Their concern for Margaret was instant and they arranged for their doctor to come at once to see her, for we had not been in their apartment for five minutes before Margaret was violently sick, followed by you know what. It was bliss to be able to pop her into a warm bath, wrap her into a soft Afghan shawl and tuck her into bed between soft, clean sheets, where she fell asleep in next to no time.

I then permitted myself the luxury of a deep hot bath, the first I had taken in ten long days. Unfortunately, I still had to climb back into my worn suit, dirty shoes and sadly laddered stockings, but these nice ladies put me at my ease. After a couple of snifters – Manhattans I seem to remember – I was smiling once more and almost back to my old self. With those on board I only vaguely recall my heart missing a beat when they told me they were taking me out to the Normandie Rooftop Restaurant for a slap-up dinner.

What a meal we had – my first decent one in Canada – and here was I like little orphan Annie who had only been used to wartime rationing in Britain. The most that could be spent on a meal in Britain at that time was five shillings. Before the war I was always known by my family as the automatic devourer, for I would will-ingly finish up anyone's leftover potatoes, but here in this beautiful restaurant the size of the portions defeated me. It appeared that I had half a cow on my plate, accompanied by a sackful of French fries and a positive vegetable garden of salad – I made the best effort I could but came to the conclusion that wartime limits must have caused my stomach to shrink!

The restaurant was like a film set from a Hollywood movie – pink-tinted mirrors everywhere and chandeliers shimmering amid satin shades. It was very exciting. Here I could choose from a menu that seemed to stretch to my toes, offering dishes that I had never even heard of, for it has to be remembered that I was but a girl in 1939. My host was tickled pink by my excitement and enthusiasm – I made an excuse to go and visit the ladies' toilets three times, just so that I could take in the beautiful plush pink decor!

Halfway through the meal a marked silence fell over the entire restaurant and it was said that Al Capone and his henchmen had come to dine. Quite frankly I had never heard of him, which again amused my host, but I do recall that whoever he was he was dressed from top to toe in white, whereas his henchmen were all in black. I remember thinking how strange it was that they all kept their trilby hats on.

We returned to the apartment to find that Margaret had been ill again. I really felt guilt-ridden that I had left her in the care of the elderly lady, but then mothers seem to spend their lives full of remorse about one thing or another. I got her dressed, and we bade our grateful farewells to this charming family and were driven to the railway station by Charles who had booked us night sleepers on the Toronto Express – this time first class! This surely had to be the last leg of our long and memorable journey.

13

OUTSIDE, LOOKING IN

George was waiting for us on the platform with his face wreathed in smiles and his arms opened wide – and into them we fell! The relief was immense and my story flowed out. As I told him all the horrors of our journey I couldn't believe that we had actually survived, somehow it all sounded so incredible spoken aloud.

My mother's only sister was Head Dietician at the Queen Elizabeth Hospital in Toronto. The plan was to go immediately to her flat in the hospital precinct. I was so excited, firstly for no longer having to cope on my own and secondly I was about to meet my aunt and benefactor from the day I had been born. I had last seen her when I was about two years old, on a trip that I had made with my mother. I only wished we were prettily dressed instead of looking so travel worn and dishevelled. We arrived and there, standing beside the steps to the entrance hall, was a bevy of ageing ladies – the matron, the bursar and my aunt. We were ushered inside where we sat down to our first colossal Canadian breakfast, which included Aunt Jemima's pancakes and maple syrup. A doctor was called to examine Margaret, for she was still a sick little girl. Having no luggage at all George and I were sent on a marathon shopping spree, with these kindly ladies only too willing to look after my aunt's great niece.

I was longing to buy, among other things, a hairbrush, for I had been forced to use only a comb while my brush was tucked away in my beauty bag in the hold. To be let loose in these super shops after those in war-torn England, where one could only make a purchase with coupons and where choice had become almost an unknown indulgence – it was indeed quite a job for George to tear me away.

Later that day we set off for my aunt's cottage on Lake Ontario at Presqu'ile Point. My introduction to the Canadian way of life was to begin at this lovely cottage. Finding somewhere to live was proving to be a problem, for building had come to a standstill during the war years and a whole new generation had grown up, married and were looking for homes. On top of all this, the returning servicemen had married overseas and were bringing their wives and children home to their mother country. The Government devised a points system and people living in large houses found that they had to offer a wing or a floor to the Government. Whilst we were all waiting to find somewhere to live we had to stay with our relatives.

I still had to face up to the problem of the wire on my teeth, so it was decided after a few weeks that I should go to Ottawa to stay with George's sister, so that I could attend a dentist. Sitting in his dental chair he took one look at me, clipped the wires and announced that they were flapping and would have to be removed. My heart missed a beat, for I was hearing what I had dreaded – the thought of false teeth appalled me. As I lay back in his chair I fully expected him to replace the wire, particularly as he said he was very busy for the next five weeks, but he didn't – he said once again that he was too busy and that I would get used to them flapping. Well, what nonsense, of course I didn't and trying to chew became a nightmare. I came out of his house and saw George waiting for me in the car a short way down the street, so I made a beeline towards him. Upon opening the door and about to tell him of my meeting with this strange dentist I was aware of excessive movement in my mouth, I could see that George trying to stifle a laugh, so I said 'Darling, what is so funny?' 'Well, look in the mirror.' I did and to my horror my three front teeth were flapping like a door off one of its hinges. It seemed that every time I spoke or moved my tongue, away went my teeth – and to think we were setting off to stay with my sister Audrey in the USA for three weeks in the morning!

It was the time of year there in the USA when everyone was holding a sweetcorn party and Audrey was being fêted in a big way, as she was the new girl in the local community. When news got around that her sister was coming to stay then a fresh load of invitations started to pour in – mostly for these sweetcorn parties. There would be mountains of juicy golden corn on the cob, served with superb salads – none of the English lettuce leaf with a slice of tomato stuck on the top of a slice of cold spam! Their salads were colourful, pretty and innovative. Spam was shipped to Britain from the USA during the war and most of us formed a great affection for it. We would serve it sliced with cold salad, but our American friends would roll their eyes in horror at our presentation, for it was common knowledge that they knew two dozen ways of serving spam and the one way that they never served it was straight out of the tin and cold!

The party I attended was a great success, though I totally failed to keep my flapping teeth under control. I was longing to tuck in to the beautiful food on offer but held back, simply because my teeth and I were not in unison! A plump, jolly lady who had obviously been watching my attempt to take the corn off the cob with a fork could stand it no longer – someone she thought must show this ill-informed English girl how to eat corn, so she came over to sit beside me. 'No honey, you don't eat your corn with a fork, but just open wide your mouth and bite' with which she gave me a demonstration. I couldn't resist it. 'Like this?' I said, and with that I took a hefty bite and my three top front flapping teeth shot up in the air and nearly bit off my nose. The look of surprise on her face was a picture. 'You see' I said, 'that's what happens when I really try to eat corn!' 'Oh! I'm so sorry honey, I had no idea you had a problem.' Whereupon we both collapsed in a fit of giggles in a heap on the grass.

George had to return to Ottawa and work, so Audrey and I were left with Margaret to while away the warm autumn days. We would puff and blow over the sultry humid heat and at times wondered if we had been mad to leave England. I knew that Audrey would settle well, but I wasn't so sure about myself, for I had always been an individualist and a bit of a loner.

We were to live in Canada for nine months, during which time I become pregnant for the second time and my bitch Judy was sent out to me as a surprise in November. I cannot with honesty say that I was not homesick or at times dreadfully lonely, for we were living a totally different way of life in unfamiliar surroundings. Also, by this time, George was becoming disillusioned with life in Canada and he too was homesick for England.

When the first snow fell I was overawed by the sheer beauty of it and Margaret and I would sit in the darkened room lit only by the warm flickering coal fire and wait for the man to come and sweep the pavement with a horse-drawn single plough. There would be jingle bells on the horse's harness and the man would be walking at the back steering it. For my little girl it was magic. We would listen for the happy laughter and jollifications as a sleigh crowded with teenagers would pass along Wilbrod

Street making their way to the mountains around Ottawa, the sleigh would be horse-drawn and they would be carrying lanterns – how I would love to have joined them.

Judy was to arrive on a bitterly cold winters' night. Unbeknown to me, George had gone to Montreal to collect her from the boat. Poor little bitch had spent two weeks on a cargo boat in rough seas to reach us. I heard George's car pull up outside and then became aware of a lot of unusual noises outside our door. He inserted his key in the lock and opened the door for Judy to enter. I was to see a very bewildered bitch come into the room. 'Judy darling' I called, I simply couldn't believe what I was seeing – it was so wonderful to have her back with me. All because my wonderful George had secretly arranged it with, of course, the help of my parents.

The winters in Canada, for those unaccustomed to the climate, seem never ending. One seems to go from the sublime to the ridiculous – the outside temperatures are sub-zero, yet inside the home it is quite the reverse, one could grow bananas in the heat! On our arrival in Canada in July the heat was excessive and the humidity was high. It seemed that Margaret and I just couldn't come to terms with it

— we were either puffing and blowing or freezing to death, with cracking ears and icicles on the end of our noses.

Due to my pregnancy, I was unable to participate in all the winter sports and Margaret was a little young to join in with all the older children, skating and sledging. Our walks in the park would inevitably result in her sitting on her pram sledge with her little blue pinched nose and ice cold hands whinging 'Mummy, I want to go home, let's go home.' So much, I thought, for our walk in the park, for I too couldn't wait to reach the warm welcome of our fire, burning brightly in the sitting room and I only had to glance down at Judy to know that these were her sentiments too.

I never could sleep in a stuffy bedroom, but here it appeared that these rooms were hermetically sealed. Winter storm windows were attached to the outside frames to keep out the inevitable stormy blasts. George would waken to find me crouching beside the window in the dead of night trying to breathe in some fresh air, for I felt as though I was suffocating. 'What on earth are you doing darling?' he would call. 'If I don't get some fresh air into my lungs I'm going to die' I would reply. I felt just like a wilting plant, my hair had started to go limp and I had the feeling that my skin was drying out like a wrinkled old prune. All these little niggles were brewing up in my mind, but I was determined not to let George become aware of them. I'd say to myself 'You'll be alright once this awful snow disappears.' Little comfort really, for I then knew that we would have to come to terms with heatwaves, mosquitoes and thunderstorms.

I read in the paper that General Montgomery was coming to Ottawa on an official visit and the prospect really excited me, for he had become synonymous with our victory in the Second World War. I dressed Margaret up warmly and she and I left the house early to make quite certain of getting a good vantage point on the official route that he was to take through the city. Imagine my amazement when I discovered that Margaret and I could have had the pick of the entire route, we seemed to be the only people lining the street to see and pay homage to this great man. Everyone else seemed to be going about their daily business. As we stood forlornly waiting for him to drive past in his cavalcade and clutching our Union Jack flags, it all became too much and I broke down and cried.

The following week Barbara Ann Scott, the pretty Canadian girl who had just won the World Figure Skating Championship, and who came from Ottawa, was welcomed home by the whole town turning out to greet her. Strange when one thinks about it, for had it not been for the inspired leadership of superb generals like Montgomery, perhaps Barbara Ann would never have been able to skate anywhere. I thought about it a great deal, and came to the conclusion this was their country after all, and deep down I realised that I would always be on the outside looking in.

Christmas – our one and only in Canada – was an interesting exercise from the culinary point of view. We had made friends with our next-door neighbours, a young couple like ourselves, with a son the same age as Margaret, called Michael. The young husband and father was the third secretary at the Australian Embassy. They suggested that we join them for Christmas Day dinner – we would do the turkey and take it round to their flat. Never before having peered inside a turkey carcass I felt that the stuffing operation was going to test my wits to the full. I had no idea which end the stuffing was to go, or indeed how to make stuffing. I found my English cook book, one that I recalled Nellie looking at when she concocted some of her 'workhouse' puddings. 'Now' I said to George, 'we will need to buy some sage and onion and it says here breadcrumbs, what kind of crumbs are those I wonder? I think they are sold in packets, I used to see Nellie using them when she fried fish.'

I duly hastened off to purchase the ingredients for my stuffing and George went off to the market to buy the turkey. Well imagine my horror when he returned with a gangling looking turkey complete with its feathers! 'George' I said, 'shouldn't you have bought one all ready to put in the oven?' There was nothing for it but to get on and attempt to pluck it. We were both at a loss to know which end we should begin, so we decided to attack it from each end, me at the neck and George at the 'Archbishops nose' end! Our kitchen, which was hardly big enough to swing a cat, took on the appearance of a slaughter house, feathers everywhere and the innards – urgh! What a smell they made and we could not open the windows for the reasons I mentioned earlier. Finally plucked, this scrawny bird began to take on the shape of a bird ready for the oven. For the final preparations we had used up a full ball of string. I had made the stuffing according to the book and, although it appeared to be like a ball of soft concrete, with a lot of pushing and shoving George and I finally managed to force it into the carcass. We felt that as it was our first attempt we had succeeded, feeling that Nellie would have given us her approval.

We timed its cooking meticulously then opened the oven door to find that the turkey had blown up at the stuffed end to look like a huge rubber space hopper. 'What shall we do darling?' I asked, thoroughly alarmed. 'There's only one thing to do and that's to make a joke about it, because it's obvious that with all the will in the world, no knife – indeed no axe – would make an impression on this incredible hulk!' We sat down on the floor and collapsed into giggles.

14

HOME

George was becoming more and more restless with the passing of every day. He would say, 'Let's go back to England, what do you think?' I longed of course to go back, but I didn't want him to make the decision on my behalf, it had to come from him, so I would try and evade the question.

One day George returned home, beaming that wonderful smile of his. 'Darling, we're going back home – I've made the application today, if we can get back before the baby is born we won't even have to pay the extra fare!'

We wrote home to give them the news and their reaction was all that we could have hoped. My father telephoned, eager and happy. I spoke to my mother as well and I knew instantly that we had made the right decision. 'Darling,' she said, 'I can't wait, I'm so excited at the thought of seeing you both and my little Margaret. I've told daddy that he managed to get Judy out to you and now he must set to work to get her shipped back!'

We all seemed to be so deliriously happy. Our plans were all completed – even to the point of arranging for Judy to travel as 'cargo' on our boat. Our passage was booked from Montreal to London's Victoria Dock. She was a banana boat of about 6,000 tonnes called the *Corales*, belonging to the Fyffe line. There were to be eleven passengers including ourselves and the journey would take two weeks. Shipping was still in short supply and cabins had to be allocated. George managed to get a cabin for Margaret and me, but he had to share with another passenger unknown to him.

I had the feeling that George's relatives thought us crazy to return to England and no doubt they put the blame fully on my shoulders. We sailed for England on 15 April 1947 – my father's fifty-fifth birthday. We sailed from Montreal and the same kind friend of George's who had met me came to see us off. We sailed down the St Lawrence and passed under the bridge at Quebec City. This time there was no magic, for it was in the middle of a cold grey day. As we neared the ocean the river became wider and wider and the remote scenery, mostly snow-covered mountains, was magnificent. I wondered if I was enjoying it more because I was going home to my beloved England?

Margaret was still as active as ever, but on this occasion I was not. I had assumed the shape of a barrel, so any chasing around the deck I left to George. There was only one deck on this little ship and the sides were more or less open, the railings being set fairly wide apart, with certainly no safely netting to stop children from falling overboard.

It was an intensely amusing trip in more ways than one. For example, George suggested that Margaret had the bottom bunk in our cabin – just in case she should roll off. I agreed wholeheartedly; however, it left me no choice but to somehow or other climb up to the dizzy heights of the top bunk and being heavily pregnant it was well nigh impossible to climb up the small ladder that they provided. We managed to get this operation down to a fine art in the end. George would stand below and push and shove until I reached the top exhausted, though more from laughing than fatigue. I found it the very devil of a job trying to rearrange myself once I was up there on this very narrow precipice, for with every movement I clonked either my head or my backside on the cabin ceiling! It was a case then of staying put until George came in the morning to get me down. Any thought of going to the loo in the night had to be put aside, I just had to hang on and wait for George. I couldn't even call a steward, for there wasn't one.

The captain, a kindly man, said we could take Judy out of her kennel in the daytime and keep her with us, a gesture that we much appreciated. On the very first day that she was to spend with us, I had left her in our cabin whilst we went to have our lunch. On returning we noticed a long trickle of water running all down the corridor, Judy had obviously been unable to contain it a minute longer and there must have been enough to fill a bucket! After that episode we could only keep her with us on the deck.

The English Channel finally came into view and in the far distance the coastline welcomed us. We travelled very close to the shoreline, sometimes only a mile out to sea. I had spent my early school days at a boarding school in Kingsdown, Kent, and I was able to actually pick out my school, situated proudly just above the shingle on the beach. I was really excited by this experience, for I so well remember as a little child sitting in my bed at night and being able to actually hear the dance music being played on a boat such as the one we were on now. I used to wonder where the boat was going to, and what sort of people were on board. Now I was seeing the picture from the other viewpoint.

Once we entered the mouth of the river Thames I felt I was home – the activity was immense with ships coming and going, brave little tugs, fishing vessels, coal ships and cargo boats. It was a beautiful morning and within a few minutes we would be docking. There is always a high and a low, it seems – my father would be waiting to take us home to my mother and Warren Farm House, but we would have to say goodbye to my dear Judy, who would have to go into quarantine kennels for six whole wretched months. I found it hard to bear the prospect of parting with her, we had after all brought this confinement upon her yet I was unable to explain that in a few months I would come and fetch her home.

'There he is,' I shouted with glee. 'Look Margaret, there's grandpa – wave darling.' We would soon be all together again, all talking at once one moment, then looking at each other and laughing happily the next. We caught up on all the news and were sad to hear that my mother's health was causing a certain amount of concern. The journey home passed quickly and before long we were turning into the long drive which would take us between our meadows down to the valley and our farmhouse. I was surprised to see my mother standing by the gate and wondered how long has she been standing there. We fell into each other's arms and the relief at being back home on the farm was tremendous.

Everything was exactly the same, it was all so comfortable. Nellie was there, the dogs were there, all the cats and last but certainly not least all our horses. Diana was away at school and Flo had gone, with her baby, to help out on a farm, the owners of which were life-long friends of my parents. We did a grand tour. Margaret had forgotten much of it, so for her it was very exciting.

After a day or two of freewheeling George had to go about finding himself a job – not an easy task, for men had been coming out of the services in vast numbers. I on the other hand had to get myself booked in once again to the nursing home. It was a long slow climb up the hill to reach it and we were experiencing a mini heatwave at the time, but still it would be lovely to be in familiar surroundings once again.

My father became Chamberlain of the City of London, and was delighted with and thoroughly engrossed in his new appointment. It was useful as well to have this new challenge to help him take his mind off the worries he had about my mother's health. He was at ease knowing that I would be at home from now on to keep an eye on her, that I was there to take care of the running of the house and – more importantly – that I was there to keep her company.

Then a disaster occurred that we could have all done without. My father had a riding accident whilst out on his early morning ride. He would leave the house at about a quarter to seven and strike out towards the Downs, on this occasion Merrow Downs. This was a daily routine and he loved it. He would come home, bathe and change into his 'city slickers', have breakfast and be away to catch the eight-twenty train to Waterloo. It was a routine that had never changed since the 1930s when I was a schoolgirl.

On this particular morning he failed to return home as he normally did. 'Muriel,' said Nellie, 'I've put the Major's breakfast in the oven, he's late this morning isn't he?' We gave it little thought, but it was a glorious morning so we came to the conclusion that he had decided to stay out longer and make the most of it. However, at nine o'clock he came in through the door looking terrible – quite grey and ashen. We realised immediately that something ghastly had happened. 'Daddy, what on earth is wrong?' I asked. 'Muriel, I've been thrown and am feeling awful, but whatever we do we must not tell your mother – can you telephone the doctor?' The doctor came right away, but it was a locum, as our doctor was still away in the Army. The locum turned out to be a big, brusque sort of woman, frightfully 'jolly hockey sticks', the sort of female I knew my father couldn't abide. She gave him the once over and said, 'You've given yourself a good old bruising, take a hot bath and you'll be all right tomorrow. I'll arrange for you to be X-rayed just to put your mind at ease.' And away she went. As it turned out my father had broken his back in three places and to think he had told me that he had managed to catch his horse and walked home leading her uphill and down dale for a good two miles!

My mother, who was upstairs, must have sensed that all was not well. When we arrived home after my father was X-rayed she came into the room and within a flash her Sister Gane persona was back on duty and in total command. In a matter of minutes she had us all running hither and thither and our elegant drawing room took on the appearance of a hospital ward. She really was a wonderful woman.

My father's major concern was that he had only just recently been made Chamberlain of the City of London. I could sense his worry – he was so anxious not to lose the threads that he had been diligently sorting out and picking up. He had a mass of high level speeches to write for the Honorary Freedoms he was about to bestow on all our wartime leaders which required access to reference libraries for he had a great deal to research. How could he possibly do this whilst stuck in a bed in Guildford? He needed his secretary and a chief clerk and he was in a turmoil, for as he said, 'I shall be judged by the way I conduct these ceremonies, Chamberlains always are and it is of the utmost importance that I create a good impression.' As he lay back on his pillow, it was obvious for us all to see that he was desolate and also in great pain. After a few silent moments he said to my mother, 'My dear, there is only one way to solve this annoying problem, I must be taken by ambulance to St Bartholomew's Hospital in London, at once, today. It is only a stone's throw away from my office and once installed there my staff and fellow officers will be able to come into the hospital and I will be able to treat it as though it were my office and carry on as usual.'

What a man, I thought, his duty to his job surpassed all concern for his broken spine. In next to no time he got his work under way not only taming the hospital, but his staff as well! He was put into plaster from neck to beam end and he remained in hospital for nearly a month.

15

THE END OF AN ERA

It was on a Friday that I came to the conclusion my baby was on the way – my mother and I were having a snack lunch together when I made the announcement. I didn't really want to go into the nursing home until George arrived home, but nature had other ideas, so I ordered a taxi, said goodbye to my mother and away I went feeling a little sad at being all alone. I received a very warm welcome upon arrival and was put into the very same bed that I had occupied on my previous visit. A bed I shall never forget, for the experience I had had underneath it with my new baby rather than the time actually spent in it! At least I should not have to dive under the bed this time, thank goodness.

The labour room was painted Madonna blue, with a beautiful large oval china plaque of the Virgin Mary and child, so positioned on the wall that as one lay on one's side puffing and blowing, she was always in vision.

Our family doctor had recently returned to his practice from his time spent in the Army and I think my baby was the first he had delivered since the outbreak of war. I'm afraid the midwives, who were nuns, thought he was somewhat out of practice and told him so in no uncertain words – I could hear all this going on in the hazy depths of my mind. I came round and realised that it was all over and as I lay there totally exhausted and soaked through with perspiration, the moment came when those magic words were uttered, 'Mrs Pushman you have a lovely little boy.' Then they handed me this vulnerable, helpless little bundle of humanity – all George's and mine. I loved the moment when a cup of tea was made and George's face appeared around the door, all smiles. We decided to call him Timothy, our son and heir. Little could we know at that happy time, that he was to be taken tragically away from us after an appalling accident when he was only twelve years old. He was so special, but was only, after all, on loan.

Dear old Puffing Billy had been retired and was housed in one of our vast barns. His companions were our fan-tailed doves and pigeons, and of course all our farmyard cats. His wheels had sunk well and truly into the muddy depths. The pigeons had created havoc with his body work, instead of a navy chassis, he was now all shades of white and grey. Two of his windows had been bashed in by some skittish bullocks who had barged their way into the barn. Our noble friend certainly should not have been allowed to sink to his present undignified state.

My father announced one day that he had decided to sell Puffing Billy. 'You can't do that father, surely?' I exclaimed. 'He is part of the family – and in any case, who on earth would want to buy him?' Secretly I hoped with all my heart that nobody would! 'Well my dears, you know my theory of old I'm sure – never become a slave to your goods and chattels.' And that was his reply.

He put an advertisement in the local newspaper saying 1927 Austin 10, goes like a bomb! The telephone never stopped ringing. He was amused by one caller, a young estate agent just demobbed from the Army, who was looking for a car to drive his prospective clients around in to show them his houses. My father found out where he lived, and advised him against making the long journey to inspect it. He said, 'Take it from me my young man, with a car like Puffing Billy you would be lucky to sell a nissen hut!'

Eventually, two men came to inspect him. My father had left instructions on what to say to the men should they appear to show interest. I went over to the barn with them. They had not got wellington boots with them, so their shoes were in quite a state by the time they had squelched across to the car. The starter button was out on a stalk of wire from the dashboard and it was a case of holding it in such a way in order to make a contact between the two wires. I explained this and one of the men got into the driver's seat. The other had opened the bonnet, the kind of bonnet that opens half at a time. He was bending over with his head well and truly tucked over the engine when – BANG! BANG! Sparks were flying in all directions and smoke belching out of every orifice! The man with his head inside the bonnet literally ran across the barn, his feet sticking in the mud with every step – his shoes had come off and were somewhere in the depths of the mud, he was as black as soot and no doubt his ears had been deafened! The other chap, in the driver's seat, sitting calm and unruffled, commented, 'I think that will have cleared it!'

There was no battery and no petrol, so they decided to come back and test drive it once they could tow it out of the mud with a tractor. I told them the price my father wanted was £80 and I fully expected them to walk away. Nothing doing – they said they would leave a deposit and be back the following day with a new battery, petrol and a tractor to tow it out of the barn!

Once old Puffing Billy had been filled with petrol he took on a new lease of life. My father, filled with curiosity asked, 'If it isn't a personal question, may I ask what you intend doing with my old car?' The reply was, 'Sir, you won't recognise it by the time we have done it up and given it a respray – in fact we'll bring it to show you, we'll get at least £300 for it!' I just wished they would stop calling him 'it', Puffing Billy was 'him' to us and always would be.

Some weeks later they did return with this resplendent motor car. We were amazed and in a way I was happy that he had been rescued from our muddy old barn. Deep down, however, I preferred to remember him in his heyday – he had so much character. But one had to give credit where credit was due and they had done a superb job.

The third time I became pregnant, I was rather run down – a common occurrence with over-worked mothers. I seemed to be running a temperature and was also losing weight. My doctor arranged for me to see a specialist at St Thomas's Hospital in London. After examining me he said, 'Mrs Pushman, my advice to you is to terminate this pregnancy.' Quite naturally, I immediately burst into floods of tears in his office, obviously startling him. 'My dear girl, it's not the end of the world.' 'Well it is to me.' I replied and on the strength of this I was given a reprieve, so long as I promised to rest and eat plenty of nourishing food.

My mother's health deteriorated noticeably and my morning sickness got steadily worse, making me feel wretched. One evening late in November I was in the kitchen ironing and talking to my mother, when I happened to notice that in trying to light her cigarette she was holding the match a good few inches away from the end of it and that her speech had become slurred. At once, I realised she was very ill. I called Nellie, 'Come quickly, give me a hand to get my mother upstairs and onto her bed.' Between us we managed somehow but we had a terrible struggle, for she fought like a tiger to stop us and her strength was almost overpowering.

I then went to find my father who was engrossed in a book in the drawing room. 'Come quickly, Mummy has had a stroke, the doctor is on his way.' Dear God, help him get here quickly I prayed fervently, for she had lost her speech totally and as hard as we tried to lay her back on her pillows she fought every inch of the way to sit up, even struggling to get out of bed. We hung onto her for all our worth, in fact we dare not let go of her for fear she would fall off the bed and hurt herself.

I have never been so frightened, everything moved at such a pace from the moment that the doctor arrived. He arranged for her to be sent immediately into a nursing home in Walton-on-Thames. It was as though a tornado had hit Warren Farm House, we were all physically exhausted and utterly desolate. I flopped into bed, but couldn't sleep and wondered just when disaster of one kind or another would cease to strike at Warren Farm House. Her life hung on a thread for a couple of days and we felt morally bound to cable Audrey in the

USA to tell her the news. She too was expecting – her second baby was due in March and her first born was only eleven months old. What a dilemma this news caused her, but with few second thoughts she cabled to say she was coming to England and would be airborne within ten hours.

Unfortunately, I started to miscarry, due, the doctor said, from trying to restrain my mother from getting out of bed. There was nothing for it but to get into bed and put my feet up. This was easier said than done, for Margaret was by now an active four year old who needed constant supervision and Tim was fifteen months. What a mess it seemed life had become. However, Nellie was a gem and somehow we struggled through, my third baby was saved and at that time this was my greatest relief.

Poor Diana, her life was to change considerably from that moment onwards. Once my mother came home there were two nurses in the house, and they would not tolerate noise of any kind, this meant that Diana from now on lived in the kitchen, far away from my mother's bedroom. I too had to keep our children quiet, though we could escape outside to run and play in the fields where only the birds could hear us.

Diana and Margaret spent entire days with our horses. Margaret had by now inherited Stjarni and I would watch her brushing and talking to him just exactly as we had done when he first arrived from Iceland fourteen years previously.

My mother was completely paralysed down her right side. Her speech was still slurred and she would become so frustrated when trying to say something to us, which we failed to understand. This independent soul had virtually become a caged bird, having to rely on her nurses to attend to her every need. Instead of lying back and accepting this appalling situation, she fought every inch of the way to be her own person, though deep down she knew she was on a losing wicket.

Some of her nurses were better than others, and I always knew which my mother didn't like, for when they weren't looking she would raise her good hand and shake her fist at them!

Nellie, the ever loyal member of the family circle, was a treasure. She used to care for my mother on the nurses' day off. She also cooked for them, though in return they were off-hand, superior and at times downright rude – especially when choosing their food. But still Nellie soldiered on, she cared for us all, but especially my mother and we were all eternally grateful. I always used to tease her by saying, 'Nellie, old Ernie has got his eye on you, I bet he will be asking you to go out to the pictures with him any day now.' He was our old gardener. Nellie would become all confused and say, 'Of course he won't Muriel, you're just pulling my leg.' She had promised my mother that she would never leave her and she never did. But eventually old Ernie did take her to the pictures and in due course they married, just as I had prophesied. Sadly Nellie died from cancer just before Christmas in 1980. She had never committed a mean turn against anyone and she will always hold a special place in my memory.

George was finally chosen for a good job in a chemical company in Cheshire and we felt that at long last his foot was on the ladder and that future prospects looked to be set fair. Of course it meant moving away from the farm once again, but this time we were only to be 160 miles away. Margaret wept bitterly when we told her, saying that she wanted to stay on the farm with Diana and Stjarni forever.

Before contemplating the move, I firstly had to go to the nursing home for the third time to produce my baby. On a glorious summer's day in June – the eleventh, we were all sitting out in the garden having a strawberry cream tea, even my mother had been brought down to join us. It was a Saturday and the restrictions on street and shop lighting were to be lifted that evening. We had all yearned for this day, for it was now ten whole years since they were officially banned. I had been looking forward to going down to the town with George once it became dark, so that we could have a thorough look at everything that was on offer in the windows.

All the while though I was aware of niggling twinges and sharp little stabs in the region of my tummy, but I had no intention of mentioning it, for I knew that the prospect of window shopping would be well and truly quashed. My other great wish was to produce our baby on my actual birthday, which was 13 June, and here it was still two days short, so I decided to keep quiet!

Being the month of June darkness did not fall until late and by nine o'clock my pains and twinges were becoming more intense. Looking at George I said, 'Darling, I think I am on the way to motherhood, so if I take my case with me can we go to the nursing home via the town and then we'll drive at top speed to the labour ward.' George was flabbergasted, 'But you never said a word about this all afternoon, when did you start to go into labour? For heaven's sake, we should go straight there now, remember this is your third baby and they have a habit of arriving more quickly – the last thing you want is to have the baby arrive in a shop doorway on Guildford High Street!'

Somehow or other I hung on – and on – as we waited impatiently for darkness to descend. George was decidedly against it, but to no avail, there was a toaster in one of the shop windows that I was determined to see. Goodbyes were said and good luck wished and we set off with my suitcase safely stowed away on the back seat. By this time the pains were coming with urgency and I was bending over clasping my rotund tummy urging it to hang on for just a few minutes longer. I managed to get out of the car and made for the shop, only an electrical shop but to me it was like Harrods in all its Christmas splendour. I stared at my toaster in wonderment, it was indeed a beauty and cost the vast sum of £1 19s 11½d.

The pains were now tearing into me every two minutes, and the contractions were increasing in strength – poor George was in a real panic to deliver me to the nursing home before it was too late. We knocked upon the heavy oaken door and a little peephole opened. 'Hello Sister, it's me, Mrs Pushman, please open up quickly.' Endless bolts and keys were rattled before I eventually crossed the threshold in a far from upright position. I gave George a big hug and away I rushed.

I loved the experience of arriving there late at night, there was a hush all around and these kindly nuns, all experienced nurses and midwives were there it seemed only to attend to me. I had a cup of tea followed by a colossal spoonful of cascara and caster oil – what a lethal combination and the final insult was that I was to be given an enema! 'Mrs Pushman' said the Sister, 'I cannot be doing with that doctor of yours hanging around, shall we get on with it by ourselves tonight?' We did and we worked well together. I was safely delivered of a bonny bouncing boy who weighed 8lb 8oz. Nigel was born on 12 June 1949 at 2.45 a.m. He was Sunday's Child – 'The child that is born on the Sabbath Day is bonny and blithe and good and gay.' Yet more reason for celebration – the toaster was delivered to the nursing home in the morning, with my mother's fondest love.

Pluto, our faithful old gentleman crossbreed, was slowly losing his hold on life and the vet, kindly but firmly, insisted that as Pluto was now fourteen years old, ninety-eight in human years, he had served a loyal and useful life and should now be put to sleep. We all stood and wept as the dear old man slowly turned his head, firstly towards the house, then to the stables and finally to take a last glimpse of his kennel under the spreading chestnut tree – home for the past fourteen years. It seemed as though he was bidding us all a last farewell in his own dignified style before being driven away forever. I honour him and would like, officially, to recall the way that he warned us to rush for the shelter by baying and wailing. It seemed as though it was his way of saying 'Hurry up, the air-raid sirens are sounding in Dorking and you only have two minutes before it will be sounding here!'

It seemed that all we held most dear was departing; Puffing Billy, old Aunt Lilah and now Pluto. I found it hard to accept. Additionally George had gone to Cheshire to start his job and only managed a quick visit home every now and again, so once more I had to come to terms with weeks of separation and loneliness. Little did I realise then that these separations were to become part of our way of life, for he chose to be on the sales side of the industry which continually involved trips abroad.

For our home George found a delightful Queen Anne farmhouse, it was in fact a Hall and had belonged to a well-known Cheshire family. It was now owned by a mud on boots farmer, who was prepared to let off eight rooms, which George's company would convert into suitable living accommodation for us until the company houses had been completed. I couldn't believe that this beautiful house had passed into such a clodhopper's hands. I used to shudder every time that I had to knock on his kitchen door to pay the rent. The family virtually lived in the vast farm kitchen and on one occasion I recall the roast sitting on the table ready for carving – still in the roasting tin. The butter was covered with blow flies and the children were wandering around with either no knickers or filthy nappies dangling down, and there, under the table was the largest chamber pot full to overflowing – it was a one-room slum in a magnificent house.

My father volunteered to drive us up to Cheshire, for George could not get home and in these days we were without a car of our own. Again it meant that I had to bid farewell to my mother. I looked at her as she lay in bed and it broke my heart – she was a prisoner in her bed and so unhappy. We had all known her amazing and untiring energy and now here she was unable to move by herself, her mental anguish at being so helpless and bedridden was imprinted in her lovely green eyes. I bent down and gave her a loving kiss and I could see the tell-tale tears in her eyes, 'I'll be back soon' I promised, but even as I said it, it struck me just how desperately lonely she must be.

My father was experiencing loneliness of another nature, he had to attend many dinners and functions in the City of London. In the past, of course, my mother would have been at his side, but now he had to attend them on his own. When he was at home he would sit beside my mother, not speaking, but just holding her hand, a simple gesture which told all.

As a father his love knew no bounds. He cared for us, and worried about us and we had always known that he would be there when we needed help or advice. He was the one who had always taken the decisions, booked our medical appointments and then taken us, sitting patiently until we reappeared. I was finding in married life that I now had to stand on my own two feet and at times I just longed for him to be near. He had the gentle knack of pouring balm on turbulent waters and making them still again.

The 15 May fell on a Sunday, it was my mother's birthday. I was sitting on our bed feeding Nigel after we had had a late and relaxed breakfast. George suddenly said, 'Hurry up now, it's Mummy's birthday and we are going to drive down to Guildford to see her, I've borrowed a car and it will only take us about four and a half to five hours. If we hurry up and leave now, we'll be in time for tea – we'll surprise her.' I chased around packing essentials, nappies, a potty, bottles of milk and orange juice for the long return journey. We piled everything into the car and off we set. The excitement was explosive, it was been a wonderful idea of George's. The bond between my mother and George was something very special, probably because his own mother had died when he was only seven years old.

The journey was not in vain, it brought happiness to all of us – particularly the element of surprise. We took the children into my mother's bedroom and she cuddled the babies as best she could – with Margaret perched on her pillow in pride of place as her special favourite, her first grandchild. We very reluctantly set off for home at ten o'clock, arriving home at three in the morning, exhausted but happy.

My father was anxious for us to spend our summer holidays down on the farm, and we didn't need much coaxing. Flo was also there to be there with her little daughter, so it had all the makings of a good holiday.

After a week or so, however, my mother suddenly became very, very ill with pneumonia. As I sat at the window of her bedroom watching the setting sun I wondered whether this bright star was to lose its light forever. I hoped not and yet strangely I hoped so, for she had told me so many times that she had longed to die. I would laugh and try to jolly her out of such morbid thoughts but now suddenly here I was with her alone in her room and I was afraid. She seemed to have no will to fight any more.

I had gone up to the vegetable garden to pick beans for lunch, when suddenly I heard a frantic call from Flo to come at once. I dropped the basket and rushed towards the house but I knew the reason for her call – Mummy had died. I had sensed it out there, as though I was aware of some inexplicable presence surrounding Warren Farm House.

Reaching the top of the stairs I met my father, my husband, Flo and Nellie converging from different directions all realising that this brave light had finally been extinguished. We silently filed into her bedroom and gazed down upon her – her face, always without a wrinkle, looked at peace. I felt emotionally drained for she, my mother, had always swept us along on the crest of the wave. Life would never be quite the same without her.

My father later wrote 'She passed suddenly to her rest, and with her went some of my hidden treasure.' These, too, are my sentiments.

If you are interested in purchasing other books published by Tempus,
or in case you have difficulty finding any Tempus books in your local
bookshop, you can also place orders directly through our website
www.tempus-publishing.com